# Information and Belief

By

Alexis Janus

This book is a work of fiction. Places, events, and situations in this story are purely fictional. Any resemblance to actual persons, living or dead, is coincidental.

© 2002 by Alexis Janus. All rights reserved.

No part of this book may be reproduced, stored in a retrieval system, or transmitted by any means, electronic, mechanical, photocopying, recording, or otherwise, without written permission from the author.

ISBN: 1-4033-4059-5 (e-book)
ISBN: 1-4033-4060-9 (Paperback)
ISBN: 1-4033-4061-7 (Dustjacket)

Library of Congress Control Number: 2002092402

This book is printed on acid free paper.

Printed in the United States of America
Bloomington, IN

1stBooks – rev. 06/19/02

# Dedication

to Cathy

# Acknowledgements

The people listed below have contributed, in one way or another, to the completion of this novel. You can thank or blame them.

My family
My friends at the Michigan Department of Corrections
Beth Ament
Mary Anderson
John Fredericks
Max Gibson
Carol Plummer
Pam Rockwell

# Chapter 1

Eric James flicked the remains of the heavily-mentholated Newport cigarette from the window of his 1988 Ford as he made a wide right-hand turn into the apartment complex. He winced as the jar from the speed bump jolted through his non-existent shock absorbers and ran through his body.

"Mother-fuckin' white trash manor," he grumbled.

The outdated red Ford with the wrinkled right fender and the torn landau top was nowhere in sight. "Nooo mamma!" he said to himself in a satisfied tone. *It pays to be screwing around with the only little bitch that has a workin' mamma instead of a welfare-collectin' soap opera-watcher,* he thought. He rolled up the window and pulled the rear view mirror to meet his gaze. He ran his fingers through his sandy blond hair, admiring the look that a $40 haircut could create. He quickly rehearsed the shy little smile that had gotten him into so many doors before, then readjusted his mirror.

He double-checked his cigarette pack to make sure the joint he had rolled late the night before was still there. He didn't really like smoking pot, but some of the girls seem to need something like that to get started. *Fuck it. Just another hoop to jump through,* he thought. *Cheaper than drinks and dinner.*

He slid the pack into the inside pocket of his suede jacket and knocked on the door. He drove his hands deep into the pockets of his jacket and turned his back to the cutting Michigan wind.

The young girl who answered the door met his grin with a blush as she dropped her gaze from his face to the doorknob. "What are you doing around here today?" Brenda Jackson asked, in an expectant tone.

"I came to see you," Eric answered.

"How did you know I'd be home?"

"My kid brother told me you two have the day off. Come on," he continued in a pleading tone, "I'm freezin' out here."

"I don't know if I should, after last time. I shouldn't…" her voice trailed off as he interrupted.

"I know," he said, in a conciliatory tone. "Things got a little out of hand. It'll be all right. We can watch videos."

She continued to nervously play with the doorknob for a moment. "Are you sure?"

"Of course I'm sure," he said. "Brenda, I've missed you."

"I'd never know it from the way you act," she replied as she stepped back and motioned him in.

He closed the door behind him and leaned down the nearly two feet needed to put himself at eye level with her. "Of course I miss you," he said as he gently kissed her forehead. "I'm your boyfriend, right?"

"Why didn't you call me after last time?"

"I've been busy. You don't know what it's like having to work every day and pay your own bills and put up with a roommate who's an asshole…" he stopped when he saw that Brenda was beginning to cry. *Shit,* he thought. "Brenda, I'm sorry. I didn't want it to be this way."

"I was afraid," she said.

"I was afraid, too," he responded. "You went on and on about how much it hurt. I thought maybe you didn't want me to come back."

"Janet said that Trish told her that you did the same thing with her sister. You went over a few times then did it with her and then never went back."

"Trish is a lyin' bitch who made up that whole thing about her younger sister because I wouldn't go out with her." He took her hands and led her to the couch. "Look," he said in a reassuring tone as he wiped the tears from her cheeks, "I know you're upset and scared because this stuff's still pretty new to ya. But it'll be better this time. It won't hurt as much, and you'll…"

"What do you mean, this time?" she asked as she pulled her hands from his. "We can't do that again."

He laughed as he took both of her hands back into his. "It's OK. There's nobody here. You don't need to play these games with me."

"No, Eric!" she protested as she tried to pull away.

He locked both of her small wrists in one hand and shoved her back to the sofa. He began to unbutton her jeans, stopping just long enough to fondle her breast.

"Don't, Eric, don't" she pleaded as she twisted one hand free and grasped at her pants in a desperate tug-of-war that ended in the painful loss of two fingernails below the quick. She screamed in pain.

He stopped pulling. "Then you take 'em off!" he yelled.

"I'll call the police if you do it," she cried as he quickly pulled off his own jeans and forced her legs apart.

He grabbed her hair by the nape of her neck, pulling her face close to his. "Bitch, quit playin' these games. It's not like we haven't done it before." He ran his hand up from her waist and under her shirt. "Take your shirt off." His voice had shifted back from yelling to coaxing. When she didn't respond, he grabbed her bra and pulled it up, exposing her breast to his hand. He fondled the nipple with his fingertips before sliding his hand back down and shoving two fingers as deeply into her as he could.

"It hurts!" she cried. "Stop!"

"It's all right," he said, his breath quickening as his excitement built. "Watch. This'll make it better." He slid down and pushed his tongue between her legs. "Isn't that good?" he said, looking up at her.

She started to cry. "No," she replied between sobs. "No."

"Fine, bitch," he mumbled as he pulled himself on top of her. "Just tryin' to help." He turned her face toward his and kissed her hard before forcing himself into her. "There. That's it," he whispered.

She closed her eyes until the pain stopped. When she opened them, she saw Eric putting his pants on. "You know," he said, "it wouldn't hurt if you'd just relax." He put on his jacket and pulled a cigarette from the inner pocket. "What are you lookin' at?" he asked defensively. When she didn't reply, he stormed from the apartment.

*These white trash bitches are all alike,* he thought as he drove from the complex. *She treats me like that, and tomorrow she'll bitch when I don't call her.*

## Chapter 2

Natalie Fisher pulled the door open, fighting its weight, the blowing wind, and the bulk of the canvas carryall strapped over her shoulder. She stepped inside, and the wind shut the door behind her. She kicked each foot to the floor several times in what is part of the Michigan winter ritual. It starts with the foot pounding, goes to the futile shoulder shrug, and ends with the tracking of cold dirty water through the dwelling.

She ran a hand through her light brown, wind-blown hair in an offhand attempt at rearranging it. At 35, she was neat and clean but certainly not obsessed with her appearance. Her work clothing tended to push the envelope of business casual. Just tall enough to escape being called short, her athletic build and assurance of movement gave her an air of confidence that bemused her at times, but that she found useful in her work.

Bits of conversation caught her ear as she passed one door-less office after another. Having worked in this building for a little less than seven months, she was still in the habit of reading the nameplates as she advanced.

*Matthews*

"It came out positive 'cause I hang with the boys," a voice inside protested. "What can I do? I gotta breathe."

"It came back positive 'cause you're using. Don't give me that secondhand smoke..."

*Jefferson*

No sound as usual. This cubical was never occupied before 8:30 a.m.

*Dowd*

"Don't give me, 'I don't have a ride.' You had a month to think about that, and..."

**Keller**

"Any police contacts or changes?"

**Moore**

"Sam and I went to Builder's Square to look for a kitchen island."
"You need to get over to Home Depot, they..."

*Information and Belief*

Natalie entered the area referred to as "the bull pen," or "rookie's row" by the senior agents. In leaner days, it had been a conference room. Now it was home to Natalie and seven other agents. The newly added dividers, cannibalized after the IRS office had moved, were placed in front of and behind each desk. Each desk was also bordered by a wall. Unfortunately, there were not enough dividers, or floor space for that matter, to provide for complete enclosure. Thus, reaching status was also referred to as "getting your fourth wall."

She scanned her desk, which had become a truly overwhelming sight. She silently longed for the days when her desk calendar was blank and free of coffee stains, when there were no yellow post-its on top of other yellow post-its, when phone numbers were neatly placed in alphabetical order in her Rolodex. As opposed to the new system of being scrawled in her own unidentifiable dyslexic style, and usually lacking any formal identification, such as a name. Realistically, she remembered that the aforementioned system of organization lasted fewer than her first three weeks with the state. In her heart, she knew that her mere existence would be a horror story to any Franklin Planner System's employee.

She smiled at her saving grace, her little Apple Mac that occupied the far left corner of the table surface. It was the same little miracle that had gotten her through four years of college, by camouflaging her spelling and grammar inadequacies. The fact that the state still didn't issue computers to its agents in 1996 seemed ironic. If she were a prisoner in a state facility, she could demand access to a computer as a basic human right.

"Good morning," she greeted the second entrant, Ed Bradner, a 29-year-old white man almost six feet tall. Today he was wearing his dark sports jacket and tan pants, and the inevitable white shirt. He owned two sports jackets and four pairs of pants, and wore them in a monotonous rotation so consistent that they all knew exactly what he was going to wear on any given day.

"Good morning," he replied. Natalie heard his chair pull back, and then several short scooting sounds as he forced it back under the desk, fighting a locked wheel the whole way. "God, I hate Friday report days," he groaned as he shuffled and stacked the yellow report forms that littered his desk.

"Why you talkin' 'bout Friday?" Edna Green responded in her normal boisterous tone. "Today's Monday. We're nowhere near Friday." The 55-year-old stocky black woman as usual sounded irritated, her weathered features set in her standard, unchanging stony expression.

Natalie was disappointed by Green's arrival. Natalie considered Ed Bradner to be one the few true intellectuals employed by the state, and she enjoyed the rare occasions when they had an opportunity to talk without interruption.

"I'm aware of that," Ed snapped back defensively. "It's just that after a long weekend I can't always remember what I was going to follow up on first. I saw over 30 felons on Friday. It's hard to remember who changed jobs, who moved, and who got arrested on new charges."

"Well, I don't ever have that problem," Green replied.

"You don't *have* a Friday report day," Natalie pointed out.

"But even if I did," Green lectured, "I wouldn't have that problem. That's the structure I was raised with."

Natalie took this as a cue to get her cup and head for the lunchroom.

"I'll keep that in mind," Ed responded in a flat tone to Green as he followed Natalie, right on her heels. "It's too early in the morning, or in the week for that matter, to listen to this," he mumbled to Natalie with a resigned chuckle.

"The burden of being the world's greatest wife, mother and former DSS caseworker is a heavy one to bear," Natalie teased as she poured her coffee.

"Especially for a divorced mother whose child visits her less than once a year," Donna Keller, a slender young blond, piped in as she entered the room.

Ed and Natalie looked at each other and tried not to spray coffee as they laughed.

"How did you know what..." Ed started.

"It's not rocket science," Keller responded. "Besides," she continued with a pause and a raised eyebrow, "in the words of our fearless leader, I'm a trained investigator."

The term 'trained investigator' had become a recent buzz phrase since the last district-wide staff meeting. The department of

*Information and Belief*

corrections' Director of Region I, Field Services was present. He was responsible for an area including the southwestern neighborhoods of Detroit, and the areas referred to locally as the downriver communities, as well as the western area of Wayne County. He had responded to a question regarding the arduous procedure for gaining access to closed files and police reports with a rather snide, "Why is it that trained investigators always want things given to them?"

"Oh, don't remind me," Ed stated bitterly, instantly recognizing the reference. He hesitated for a moment and considered changing topics. There were days when he couldn't stand to hear himself. But he had always found that when he felt personally attacked, he would lash out verbally. Since being hired by the state a little more than three years prior, he felt attacked frequently. "But do you know what really burns me about a crack like that?"

"A crack like what?" Kay Elds asked tentatively as she entered. Natalie smiled; she liked Elds. At 45, the short, almost-190 pound white woman was confident, cheerful, and quite comfortable with her appearance. When Natalie had first started working in Corections, Elds had showed her the ropes and politics of the office.

Elds was just steps ahead of Joan Ballard, a 30-year-old white woman with dark brown hair and deep-set brown eyes. Slightly shorter than Natalie, she was slightly heavier.

"What did we miss?" Joan asked.

"Nothing. I think Ed is about to relive the last district-wide," Natalie replied as she turned her attention back to Ed.

"What baffles me," Ed continued, "is that a man in his position had to have gone to college. And most of us who went to college eventually took at least one leadership class." He paused for effect. "What school of leadership teaches you to build team cohesion through insults?"

"I can almost picture him in college," Natalie said. "He was that little guy at the back of the class taking copious notes and learning nothing." She added a little comic relief by pantomiming a person with a notebook two inches from her nose scribbling feverishly.

The laughter was interrupted by a few seconds of loud static followed in stark contrast by a soft voice announcing, "Mr. Jefferson…Miss Keller…Miss Green…You have clients."

"Clients," Kay mumbled as she left the room. "Kind of sounds like we're stockbrokers instead of probation officers."

"Now that would make your mother proud," Joan replied as she followed her out.

"Fisher, there's something I've been meaning to ask you," Bradner said as he rose from his chair. "Do you remember that gay guy I was interviewing last week?"

Fisher laughed. "I knew you were going to ask me about that. You're going to ask me to speak for my people again, aren't you?"

"Well, you're the only gay person I know that doesn't get offended by questions." He tentatively added, "You aren't offended, are you?"

"Not at all. Exactly what do you want to know?"

"He said that one of the local gay groups is suing the State Police over the sting operations at the Route 275 rest areas. I don't understand, how is having sex in a public restroom a gay issue?"

"Well, from what I've read and heard, the issue is not exactly aimed at the right to have sex in a public restroom. It has to do with unequal enforcement. Usually, if a man and a woman get caught having sex in, let's just say, some indiscreet place, the police give them a lecture and tell them to get their clothes on and get the hell out of there. When people of the same sex are caught, it usually results in the felony charge of gross indecency between males. Or I guess gross indecency between females, although that charge is a lot less common."

Natalie had grown accustomed to fielding these types of questions. She was sure that by this time everybody in the office knew she was a lesbian. There had never been any grand announcement. Natalie just never made a point of hiding any aspect of her life. She would frequently talk about her life, which included, among other things, a girlfriend. Eventually, a few brave people asked. The grapevine took care of the rest.

"Oh...wait," Elds interrupted as she briskly returned. "I almost forgot. Got a gift for ya, Fisher," she said coyly as she tossed the file on the lunchroom table and let the momentum glide it in Natalie's general direction.

Natalie eyed the offering with suspicion. "It doesn't look like the pony I've been asking for since I was a kid."

"A little more along the lines of what the pony left behind," Kay responded with a smile. "Cooper told me to reassign this pre-sentence investigation to you."

"Why?"

"I'll explain later."

"Oh great. CSC 3rd," Natalie groaned.

"Don't worry," Kay said in a reassuring tone. "The referral form says the judge is looking at counseling and HYTA."

"HYTA, on a rape?" Natalie said in an uncertain tone. "The Holmes Youthful Trainee Act is usually reserved for first-time offenders who commit non-violent crimes. Why would the judge consider giving a rapist an expungement of his criminal record?"

"Exactly," Kay responded. "It's probably just one of those 17-year-olds with a 15-year-old girlfriend things."

"Never underestimate the wrath of a young girl's mom," Natalie said as she leafed through the file. "I wish they'd still put the investigator's reports in here. I hate going into an interview blind."

"Never fear," Kay said in a placating tone, "I'm sure the rapist will be happy to tell you exactly what happened."

## Chapter 3

Eric James ran a comb through his hair and studied his reflection in the mirror. He smiled briefly, then stopped. *Too tense around the eyes,* he thought. He tried again. *That's better. An innocent smile. Don't want to look too cocky, like I already know what's gonna happen. My lawyer told me they hate that.* He replayed the conversation in his mind.

"Little bureaucrats like to think they have some power," Charles Hayden had warned as he pushed Eric's file in his briefcase, in exchange for his day planner.

"Why should I go kiss some probation officer's ass?" Eric replied in a hostile tone. "We've already got the judge with us, right?"

"We don't have anything yet," Hayden shot back. "You paid me a lot of money, but it won't do you any good if you don't listen and do what I tell you, when I tell you." He looked up from his planner at the blank stare of his client. He sighed. "Come with me," he snapped impatiently as he led his client down the hall.

Hayden stuck his head into three occupied rooms before finding one vacant. They entered and sat.

"Today," Hayden told Eric, "you pled guilty to three counts of CSC 3rd. Do you know why I'm always careful to call it CSC 3rd?"

"No," Eric replied.

"Because the word rape makes people's blood boil."

"There was no rape..." Eric started.

"I've already heard it, and frankly, I don't have time to stroll down memory lane with you on this one. The point is, I've got the judge asking all the questions we want him to ask. Why did she let you in? If she had sex with you before, why did she say no this time? He's looking at her school record and her home life."

"But that's what I said," Eric protested. "He's with us. Hell, she didn't even show up."

"She was advised of the plea by the prosecutor. She didn't have to show up."

"But again..." Eric started.

*Information and Belief*

"But again," Hayden interrupted, "we want the judge to keep looking there. The pre-sentence report will be his chance to look at you…your record…your home life."

"There's not much for them to find," Eric said.

"I hope not. The judge had his clerk put his sentencing thoughts on the referral. But…now pay attention…we did not enter into a binding sentencing agreement. Now, if you don't blow it, that should be a formality. This is an old judge's trick. He tells the probation department what he wants them to recommend. That way, if anything goes wrong…"

"Goes wrong?"

"Like you rape someone else two weeks after he puts you on probation. Then he can blame his decision on their recommendation. Elected officials know how to cover their asses."

"But he's the judge, so they gotta go along, right?"

"They don't *gotta* do anything, son." Hayden emphasized the word "gotta" in the hope that his young client would realize just how stupid it sounded. The effort was wasted. "Just don't give them a reason to dig too deep or care too much, and you'll be fine. You've got nothing on LEIN and you come from a good family. Be on time, wear a tie, and look sorry."

"I can do that."

"I hope so," Hayden said with another sigh as he snapped his briefcase shut and led his client out of the room.

## Chapter 4

Natalie returned to the desk with the newly acquired file. She withdrew the referral form and examined it more closely. D11 appeared in the bottom left corner as the referring district court. *Well, that's convenient,* she thought. With Trenton being her home town and only 30 minutes away, it would be a handy stop on the way home, and a good excuse to slide out a few minutes early.

She peeked at her watch: 8:35. She picked up the phone with one hand as she fumbled with her Rolodex with the other. Taylor, Gwen; Trenton PD, Trenton. *Great command of the alphabet,* she thought as she pulled Gwen's old phone number from the deck. She smiled at the fleeting memory of the day Gwen had convinced her to move from her two-bedroom apartment in Ann Arbor into the "fixer-upper" ranch-style home on the Trenton's southern edge. Maybe convincing was not a good word. It took very little persuasion. The two had been lovers for a little less than a year by the time the offer arose.

"We really need to make a decision on this soon," Gwen had prodded. "Your lease is up next month."

"I know," Natalie responded as she lifted Gwen's cat, Rowdy, from her resting place against Gwen's legs. Rowdy released a pathetic whine as she dashed off. "I guess she told me."

"You kicked her out of her favorite spot," Gwen said as she pulled Natalie under her arm.

"It's my favorite spot too," Natalie replied as she leaned into the warmth that she considered to be the essence of the other woman.

"I was talking about where you want to live."

"So was I."

An obnoxious beeping, followed by the recorded announcement, "If you'd like to make a call, please hang up and try again," pulled Natalie back to the bull pen. *You're a real life Walter Mittie,* she thought as she dialed the Trenton PD and mentally prepared her standard greeting.

"Trenton PD, Officer Mitchell."

She quickly launched in. "Hi, this is Natalie with State Probation. How are you?" she asked brightly.

"I'm just fine," the voice responded flatly, and with little sincerity.

"Good. I'm calling because I've been assigned a pre-sentence investigation on a defendant arrested out of Trenton, and I need the investigator's write-up."

There was a pause, and Natalie held her breath. One of three things could happen. In the best-case scenario, she would be given the investigator's name and transferred to his line. The worse response would involve a lecture about the expense and wasted time spent duplicating a report that has already been sent downtown and, in any sane system, would have been forwarded to Probation with the file and referral. If the officer answering the phone has a truly sadistic sense of humor, he'd transfer Natalie to Records. They would usually require you to come in person, with ID, so they could tell you the name of the investigator who, no matter what time of day you arrived, had just stepped out. Natalie was sure there was some conspiracy between the Records clerks and the investigators to perfect the timing of this event.

She heard the clicking of fingernails on a keyboard and released a quiet sigh of relief when he announced, "You'll be talking to Detective Lieutenant Cash." She was abruptly switched to another line. Two quick rings were followed by a series of male grunts that vaguely sounded like, "Detective Bureau."

"Hi, this is Natalie with State Probation. Is Detective Lt. Cash available?"

"This is Cash," the voice responded.

"I'm doing the pre-sentence report on one of your cases and I was wondering if I could get a copy of your write-up?" The defendant's last name is James. First name..."

"Eric," Cash said without hesitation.

Natalie winced. *That's never a good sign*, she thought.

"We sent a copy downtown, ma'am," he stated flatly. "It was in the court file. I reviewed it when it looked like he might not take a plea."

"Yeah, I'm sure it was," Natalie responded. "The problem is that they take the write-up from the court file, copy it, and then hand-write a referral. Then they send us the referral, but not your report."

"They what?" he asked in disbelief.

"They take it out," Natalie explained. "Then they put it in a pile, along with all the other cases disposed of that day. When the pile gets big enough, someone...and at this point I should let you know that the someone is usually the person who gets the most tired of tripping over them...takes them to a black hole we call the write-up room."

The officer started to laugh. "So what happens to them when they get there?"

"No one really knows," Natalie said in her best ghost story-telling tone. "We've never seen one that was connected with a case we were actually working on."

"The good news is," Ed interjected loudly from the other side of the office, "they just found that Little Lindbergh Baby paperwork."

"I heard that," Cash laughed. "You Detroit folks'll have that whole Manson mess cleared up any time now, huh?"

Natalie could tell she was gaining a sympathetic ally. "Did you ever read *Catch 22*, Lieutenant?"

"I was in the military, ma'am. I *lived* Catch 22."

"Well, the rumor in Corrections is that the department gave Joseph Heller a part-time job designing our system."

Natalie relaxed. She could feel the pity flowing through the phone lines. This was a man who could appreciate the truly ridiculous. In other words, this was a veteran Wayne County employee and resident. "So," she concluded, "is there any chance that I can pick up a copy on my way home tonight?"

"I'll do ya one better," he responded. "What's your fax number?"

Natalie leaned back in her chair and smiled. This must be what the guy felt like who bought Manhattan for a handful of beads.

# Chapter 5

"Come on, Sophia," Eric yelled as he pushed the knot of his tie up the Rayon base and as close to his neck as possible without cutting off all oxygen to his brain. "We can't be late."

"I'll be ready in just a minute," replied the faint voice from the walk-in closet. "I can't find my other tennis shoe."

"Tennis shoe!" he snapped in a reproaching tone. "What are you trying to do?"

"What do you mean?" she asked as she emerged from the closet.

"Jeans, a tee shirt, and tennis shoes," he said with a roll of his eyes. He walked around the petite girl and scanned her from top to bottom. "Jeans, a tee shirt, and tennis shoes," he repeated.

"What?" she asked quietly as she stared at the floor.

"I thought you loved me," he admonished her as he continued to walk around her.

"I do love you," she said weakly.

"You love me," he said sarcastically. "If you love me," he continued as he put his hand to her chin and lifted her head until her eyes met his, "then why are you trying to put my ass in prison?"

"In prison!" she gasped. Her brown eyes grew large and filled with tears.

"Where else?" he said in a gentler, almost pleading voice. He took her hands in his and led her to the bed. The two sat as he continued. "We both know I didn't do anything, right?"

"Yes," she responded without hesitation.

"OK. Now I've gotta walk in and look like the kind of guy who didn't do anything. I've got to look like the kind of guy who has it all. A good job, a stable life...all that kinda stuff."

"But," she asked tentatively, "what does that have to do with my wearing jeans?"

Eric could feel his heart start to pound and his face turn warm. On any other day, he would never take this kind of back talk. But he knew he couldn't afford to get into a fight today. He took a breath and did his best to keep the anger out of his response. "They think I sleep with teenie boppers. So don't you think it's important for you to look as far from a teenie bopper as possible?"

Sophia felt her palms start to sweat. There were other things she wanted to know. Why did they care what she looked like? Were they going to talk to her? What should she say? But she knew that feeling in the pit of her stomach. The one that told her that one more question would be one too many. She knew how angry that made him. And when she got him angry, sometimes he just couldn't control himself.

She walked to the closet, removed her job interview dress from the far corner, and held it in front of herself. She felt the muscles around her shoulders relax as he smiled his approval.

# Chapter 6

"Aw," Natalie groaned as she entered the copier room. It was an all too familiar sight. Three people were lined up at the fax machine. "Say it isn't so," she pleaded.

"Fraid so," the steno, Tracy Mills, responded. "The copier's been down since yesterday afternoon."

"But when you make copies on this old fax," Natalie stated, "it can't receive."

"If I let this stuff go, I'm gonna get behind," Tracy replied as she fed another amended order through the top and pushed the over-ride button.

Natalie made every effort not to let her voice betray the frustration she was beginning to feel. "I can understand that you sometimes have to use the fax in a pinch when you have to copy something important that has to leave the office right away. But to tie it up with unsigned amended orders..."

"I don't know what you think is so unimportant about these," Tracy responded defensively. "You don't want an auditor pouring through your file and not find this pending amended order."

"First of all," Natalie said, "everything that goes out today will be signed by the judge, and be back in its original form well before the audits. This is December, and the caseloads won't be audited until September. Secondly, the amendment requests you're doing right now haven't been signed by the supervisor yet. So you're just going to jam our boxes with three copies of the same amended order in different stages..."

The two were interrupted by a series of beeps.

"Now look what you've done," Tracy snapped. "The incomings have logged on." She tapped the option button several times. "We're locked out" The disappointed crowd shuffled off.

"Sorry," Natalie replied. Her smile betrayed any sense of sincerity she may have attempted to feign, in an effort to remain politically correct. She read the screen of the antiquated machine. Incoming: 11 pages. *Damn*, she thought. *That's way too long to be mine.* She was about to leave the room in defeat when the cover page caught her eye. The words TRENTON PD pulled her back. It was, in fact, sent to her attention from Det./Lt. Cash. A note in the comments section read, "Your report, plus some interesting reading."

She checked her mailbox, third row across and second from the top, while the pages slowly fed through the machine. The mailbox contained three faxed copies of the same memo. One was made to the attention of the office manager. He had made a copy and distributed it among all the staff. Then, to add the personal touch, he personally wrote a note to all the supervisors on his staff to make sure that *their* staff was made aware of the memo. This prompted Natalie's ever-vigilant supervisor to run a copy for his staff. This action resulted in Supervisor Barns, who was not to be outdone, running one for the entire staff. Thus Natalie had three identical copies.

The memo advertised a community service project. Since most judges had found it to be politically advantageous to order probationers to do community service, new referrals were always appreciated. Unfortunately, this project had ended two weeks ago.

Natalie threw all three sheets out, and checked the progress of the fax machine. Page 8 of 11.

"I saw that," Joan Ballard scolded. "Throwing away the words of our fearless leader," she continued sarcastically as she tossed the identical three sheets from her box in the trash.

"What a waste," Natalie added.

"All the paper we use," Joan said with a sigh. "Just think how many trees died to supply this office with paper for one day."

Natalie pulled the now-completed fax transmission from the tray. "Hopefully, not in vain," she replied absently as she scanned the pages. Then, "What the hell is all this?"

"Fisher, it worries me that you look confused every time I see you," Supervisor Barns remarked as he entered the room.

"That's because every time you see me, I'm here," she replied. "We've got a cause and effect thing going. Pay attention."

"That's very funny," he replied flatly. After 10 years of the gallows humor of Corrections, he had become immune to it. People needed to blow off steam, and this was the most harmless way he could think of.

"What do you make of this?" Natalie asked as she handed him the documents.

*Information and Belief*

After examining the papers, he stated, "You've got four different write-ups on the same guy. How many dockets?"

"One docket, three counts," she replied.

"Well," he said thoughtfully, "that doesn't account for this. It looks like you've got three different victims. One docket and three counts usually means same victim and three crimes."

"I guess I could check the arrest dates against the conviction and referral slip."

"That should work," he confirmed. "But if these are pending cases, this guy is in a world of hurt. Those are all CSC complaints."

"They can't be pending," she speculated. "He'd never be out on bond."

Barns shrugged as the two went their separate ways down their respective halls. He thought Fisher was going to make a good agent if she'd learn to be a little more patient. Let things unfold in their own time. He considered her to be a prime candidate for burnout. She needed to learn that questions lead to more questions, and more questions lead to more work. You need to understand that there's a time to quit asking. Someone should take the time to teach her. Then he remembered his own philosophy. Don't rush in. Someone will teach her. If he waited long enough, it would be someone else.

*Alexis Janus*

# Chapter 7

Natalie hurried across the bull pen when she realized that her phone was one of the three ringing. She tossed the reports in the top of the three stacking trays on her desk and snatched the receiver up in a vain attempt to beat the answering machine. Too late. "Hello," she heard her voice say. "This is Ms. Fisher, Probation Agent for the Michigan Department of Corrections." She winced. She hated the sound of her voice on tape. "I'm here," she said over the recorded message. "Give me a chance to turn this thing off." The message droned on. "Please understand that a phone call does not constitute a report to this office and any attempts to reschedule must be discussed with me personally." She hit the stop button. "OK, that's got it."

"Is Ms. Fisher in?" the caller inquired.

"This is Ms. Fisher," she responded.

"Oh," the man replied. "Well, this is Danny. I was wondering…"

"Wait…hold on," she interrupted. "Danny who?"

"Danny…Danny Stalk."

"Ahh, Mr. Stalk," she said cheerfully. She always tried to keep her tone polite, friendly and professional. At times, this seemed like a balancing act that would challenge the great Wallendas. "What can I do for you?"

"Well," the young voice stammered, "I'm supposed to report to you tomorrow…and…I know you said I needed to have a restitution payment, but the thing is that a lot of things came up this month. I was wondering if I could wait and report in two weeks after I get paid again and…"

"Mr. Stalk," Natalie interrupted in the firm tone she had mastered over the past year. "Your report day is tomorrow. That is the day you will report. Secondly, you need to report with your payment. Things come up for people every month. That doesn't excuse your obligation to the victim, or…"

"But my lawyer said that if I'm on probation for two years then I have two years to do this stuff," he replied defensively.

She kept her voice calm. She had learned early that people feed off the anger of others, and she was not in the mood to get into a shouting match this early in the morning. "Mr. Stalk, I don't know

*Information and Belief*

what your lawyer told you. I only know that you did $800 worth of damage to the victim's car. When you add that to the $165 court costs per year and the $360 supervision fee per year assessed by the court, that means you need to be paying at a rate of..."

"You don't seem to understand," he replied in a pleading tone. "I've got a car repair of my own. If I don't work, how do you expect me to pay all that money?"

Natalie was growing impatient, and did not want to get drawn into the long rationalization she knew was coming. She hated to do this. But she knew she had to move in for the kill. And nothing hurt the average felon more than cold, hard fact.

"Mr. Stalk. As I recall when I did this investigation, you trashed the car of a young mother of two who lost her job that day because she couldn't get to work. I don't remember anything about you asking if it was a convenient time in her life to lose everything she'd worked for."

There was a pause. "But my lawyer said..."

"Then your lawyer can stand with you again before the judge and explain his position, sir," she replied curtly. "After all, I'm not the be-all and end-all of the system. If you're confident that the judge will side with you, then don't come in tomorrow and don't make your payment. I'll send in a violation of probation warrant request. You two can go back before the judge and..."

"Wait a minute," he said apprehensively. "Don't do that. I don't want to go back before the judge."

Natalie sensed her moment and changed her tone from confrontational to amiable. She lowered her voice. "Then we both know what you need to do. Just take care of business. Come in when you're supposed to and bring your payment."

Another pause. "I'll do what I can," he replied.

"It's all in your hands, sir," she replied. "I'll see you tomorrow."

"I'll try," he replied before abruptly hanging up.

"When did people forget about saying good-bye?" she mused aloud as she returned the phone to its cradle.

"Imagine that," Donna Keller interjected slyly. "A felon with bad phone etiquette."

Ed Bradner laughed. "I've got it. This is how we'll make our new careers. Picture it. A felon's book of etiquette." He rolled his chair to the left to view his audience from around the partition as he continued. "For example, how long after a car theft do you wait before sending the thank-you card to the victim?"

"And don't forget the added tips on how to make the note untraceable," Donna added.

"A felonious occupation is noooo excuse for rudeness," Natalie added in her best Emily Post voice. Although it sounded more like Julia Childs, it still got a laugh.

"Ms. Green...Ms. Keller and Ms. Fisher, you have clients," the disembodied voice softly announced.

Natalie looked at her watch: 8:55. True to form for a CSC. He's early. She thought about getting him from the lobby and starting the interview. Then she remembered the reports in her tray. She didn't like to keep people waiting needlessly. She was unlike other agents, who felt this an important part of the 'showing them who is in charge' process. But she decided to take advantage of the fact that she actually had a report. She could read it in five minutes and still treat him with the courtesy of being on time.

TRENTON PD INVESTIGATOR REPORT

DATE OF COMPLAINT: 12/5/95
TIME OF COMPLAINT: 8:05 PM
LOCATION: 6171 Temple Square, Trenton, MI
VICTIM NAME: Brenda Jackson
AGE: 13
ADDRESS: 6171 Temple Square, Trenton
COMPLAINANT'S NAME: Wanda Jackson    AGE: 27
ADDRESS: Same

COMPLAINT: CSC 3

SUSPECT(S): James, Eric
AGE: 20
ADDRESS: 42 W. Pack, Wyandotte, MI

RESPONDING OFFICER(S): P.O. Gates
INVESTIGATOR: D/LT. Cash

*Information and Belief*

On 12/5/95 at approx. 8:05 P.M., P.O. Gates was dispatched to the above location. Upon arrival, contact was made with complainant Wanda Jackson. Complainant reported that her 13-year-old-daughter had informed her that she had been sexually assaulted on or about 11/24/95 sometime between the hours of 10 a.m. and 11:30 a.m. She further reported that the assailant was known to the victim to be Eric James. Complainant was unsure as to the suspect's address, but states he may reside in Woodhaven, MI. A subsequent LEIN/SOS reflects the address listed above. At this time, the case was turned over to the Detective Bureau.

On 12/6/95 at approx. 9:05 a.m., the victim was transported to Trenton PD by her mother. She was interviewed by D/LT Cash and provided the following written statement:

"Eric came over in the morning while my mom was at work. I was home because it was the day after Thanksgiving. He said he knew I was home because his brother and I are in the same class at Trenton Jr. High. I knew I wasn't supposed to let him in, but I did so we could watch videos and stuff. We sat and talked for a while and then he started talking about wanting to have sex. I told him no but he kept telling me it was OK. He unbuttoned and unzipped my pants. He had trouble getting them off me and he yelled at me to take them off. I was scared because he yelled at me so I did. Then he took his off and pushed me back on the couch. He started feeling my chest and told me to take my shirt off. I didn't. He put his hand between my legs and put his fingers in me. I told him it hurt and he said he could make it better. Then he got off me, pushed my legs apart and put his tongue between my legs. I told him to stop and pulled away. I tried to get up then but he pulled me back down. Then he said, "Fine, Bitch. Just tryin' to help." Then he got back on top of me and put his penis into me. When he was done he got dressed and acted like nothing happened. When I wouldn't talk to him, he got mad and left."

Upon subsequent verbal interview, the victim stated that she had told the suspect, "I'll call the police if you do it." When asked re: his response, the victim disclosed that she and the suspect had engaged in consensual sexual intercourse on one occasion. She stated that she had not said anything about this earlier because he said no one would believe her if they knew. She also stated that she was afraid that her mother would blame her if she knew.

On 12/6/95 at approx. 1:10 p.m., the suspect was contacted by phone and informed of the allegations. He initially denied having known the victim. After being confronted with the fact that other acquaintances would be contacted, he admitted that he knows the victim and that he did have sex with her on several occasions. However, he stated that he believed her to be 17 years of age and that all sexual contact was consensual. He agreed to report to the Trenton PD on 12/7/95 and provide a written statement.

On 12/7/95 at approx. 9:05 a.m., the suspect contacted this office by phone and stated that, upon the advice of counsel, he would not be making a statement.

RECOMMENDATION

Based on information and belief, a warrant is recommended on three (3) counts of CSC 3rd degree.
Count #1: Digital penetration. Count #2: Oral Penetration. Count #3: Penile Penetration.

Natalie had barley finished the last page of the first report when she was interrupted by the soft voice, "Ms. Green and Ms. Fisher, you have clients."

Natalie leaned back in her chair and flipped to the next page. *He can wait*, she decided.

*Information and Belief*

# Chapter 8

Eric was uneasy. He never liked waiting, but this was worse than usual. Why did he have to wait with these people? Its not like he was some drug addict, or stickup man. Some stupid bitch doesn't want to get grounded by her momma and the next thing you know, you're sitting with the scum of the earth suckin' up to someone who works for the state 'cause they can't get a real job.

"Who you got?" asked the middle-aged man sitting across from him.

Eric was pretty sure this question was meant for him. He didn't respond. The lobby was small, and it was filling up fast. Mismatched chairs lined three of the walls and bordered the one small table in the middle on three sides, with the fourth being pushed against the wall, creating a tight walkway. There was only room for four chairs at the table. The rest of the people were filling out forms on their laps.

"Who you got?" the man repeated. The tone was more insistent.

"What do you mean?" he asked as he leaned back, putting his arm around Sophia.

"What agent you got?" the man clarified.

Eric removed his arm from behind Sophia's chair and turned over the manila envelope in which he had carefully stored all the papers that were on the 'List of items needed for the pre-sentence interview.' The name Fisher was neatly written on the top right hand corner. He looked up at the questioner. The man hadn't shaved in several days and was dressed in oily coveralls. In any other setting, Eric wouldn't give this bum the time of day. "Fisher," he replied.

"This ain't Fisher's report day," a black man with a thick southern accent blurted out from his seat at the far wall.

"He's not here for a report," the first man said with a knowing smile. "Look at him with his little bundle of goodies," he mocked as he pointed to the envelope. "The puppy is here for a pre."

"What are you talking about?" Sophia asked defensively. Eric cut her in half with a look, and she instantly wished she were anywhere else.

"Us who report," the black man explained, "we're already on probation. Your boy there, he still gots to go back to court. So they're doin' the report and tellin' the judge if they think he should be on probation or not. 'Dat calt a pre. Short fo' somethin' like...Pre-jail report."

"Pre-sentence report," another voice corrected.

"He ain't got nothin' to worry about," a Hispanic man voiced in an assuring manner. "I mean, I've heard she can be a real pain in the ass like any of 'em. But she's no Ms. Green."

This statement was followed by a chorus of groans.

"Green's the worst," the first man concurred. "She's known for making up her own rules as she goes. She'll violate your probation just to get rid of some work before her vacation."

"Keller can be a real ballbreaker," another added. "She's got me droppin' every report."

"Droppin'?" Eric asked.

"You know," the black man teased. "Piss in the cup."

"With The Big Man right over your shoulder, eyein' your dick," another complained.

"What?" Eric barked.

"Get used to it, son," the first man counseled. "They watch to make sure you don't try to switch bottles or put something in to cover up the drugs."

"I don't do drugs," Eric stated defensively. "I'm not here for anything to do with drugs. They can't make me do that."

"Everyone drops for the pre," the first man stated. "If you drop clean, you might not have to drop while you're on probation. But, if you give 'em a reason to think you have a problem...you know...like tellin' 'em they can't make you drop, you'll be pissin' in a bottle in front of an audience for the next few years."

# Chapter 9

Natalie took her empty coffee cup back to the lunchroom for a refill. Three graphic rape accounts were about all she could take, and it was only 9:15 a.m. The second two were a lot like the first. Little, trusting girls. All under 14, and all from the same housing project in Trenton. The primary difference was in the warrant recommendation. The latter two had decided that they didn't want to testify. No warrant was recommended.

She thought back to her days as an intern at the local domestic violence shelter. Since it was a small, understaffed facility she had to work in all the programs, from domestic violence to sexual assault. For three months, she and another worker facilitated the teen sexual assault group. She had heard a hundred stories just like the ones she had just read. In one sense, she was used to it. Over the course of her two years there, she had learned the needed counseling survival skill of emotional separation. She developed a mental game called "reflect back."

The idea came from the monotonous process learned in empathy classes, where you slightly rephrase the other persons statements so they know you're listening actively and understand what they are saying. When she was doing this, she would imagine that she truly was a mirror. Nothing gets through a mirror. That's not what a mirror is there for.

But some things she never got used to. Like a person's never-ending ability to convince themselves of whatever was most convenient to believe. The look on a child's face when mom decided they didn't need counseling anymore. "The whole thing just got blown out of proportion. He only acts like that when he drinks. He's going to AA now. We'll be safe. He earns a good living. The children need a father."

"I'm telling you," Dowd stated vehemently as he entered the room, "he's the stupidest little shit I've ever seen."

"Stupid like a fox," Bradner countered.

"What kind of an idiot walks into a store, shoves five cartons of smokes in his shirt, and tries to just walk out?"

"The kind of idiot that must have gotten away with it a hundred times before he got caught," Jefferson replied. "Look at it from a business perspective. Any multi-million dollar business that could make that kind of profit with that minimal a risk would jump at it."

The blank look on Dowd's all-American apple-pie face revealed that Bradner was still two steps, and at least 20 IQ points, ahead of him.

"Let's look at it this way," Bradner continued in an attempt to clarify his point. "Five cartons of smokes at $22 apiece. That's $110 a day. And that's if you only hit one store a day. The only dumb thing this guy did was take name-brand smokes instead of generics."

"What's the difference if he's not going to pay?" Dowd asked.

"The name brand is what pushed him into the felony range, since they price out over $100. If he'd of been caught swiping Basics, he'd be in district court on a misdemeanor instead of playing with the big boys in Circuit Court on a felony." Bradner fed the vending machine $.55 and selected the ginger snaps before continuing. "Anyway, my point is, on a small retail fraud, he'll get one year probation, tops. That's $165 court costs, and since he has no real job, he'll only be assessed $120 in supervision fees for the year."

"That's a lot of money to some people," Dowd said defensively.

"It's three runs to the store for your guy," Bradner concluded.

"Mr. Jefferson and Ms. Fisher, you have clients," the gentle voice prompted.

Natalie returned to her desk with a fresh cup of coffee, opened the clean, new file, and began organizing the forms. This was a ritual she had learned from Kay Elds when she had helped Natalie along on her first interview. It was her way of keeping a psychological edge. Put things in the order you're going to ask them. Don't start with his version of the offense, or his prior criminal record, even though that's the way the interview forms are in the book. You don't want to start with an argument and spend the first half hour listening to why his attorney/the judge/the victim/the system/you…screwed him. Start with the basic information form. Something benign will put him at ease. Most important: Don't let the defendant lead the interview.

She put the papers, in their new order, back into the file and cleared the remaining clutter from the surface of her desk. She was ready.

# Chapter 10

Natalie glanced from side to side when she exited the hall and entered the lobby. A short, blond woman beat her to the sign-in sheet by two steps. She sized up the crowd, as was her habit when she was stuck out there.

Three young guys in plaid shirts, one with his pant leg rolled up. All in what seemed to be an endless state of inhaling in order to maximize the size of their chests. Gang members. It use to be bandannas. Now it's those plaid shirts. She laughed to herself as she thought they looked more like urban lumberjack wannabes than gang-bangers.

Several familiar faces. Green's "mid-life crisis crack dealer," as he had come to be known in the bull pen, sat at the table with an older black man and a young Hispanic.

Another young guy was sitting close to a young, dark haired girl. His hair looked freshly cut. She looked like she would, at this moment, make herself invisible if she could. He was wearing a tie, was clean shaven, and was holding the telltale manila envelope. That was probably her interview.

The blond stepped aside. Natalie searched the sign-in sheet for her name. *Green is really backed up,* she thought as she ran her finger quickly over six names registered for her co-worker. One was registered for her.

"Mr. James," she called.

The young man with the new haircut popped up. "That's me," he said. He flashed an engaging smile and continued, "But you can call me Eric."

Natalie sensed she needed to set the tone immediately. "That's very kind, sir. But we're not on a first name basis here," she responded as she held the door separating the lobby from the offices and motioned for him to enter. She took special care to make sure that her voice didn't sound harsh or demeaning.

"Oh," he acknowledged tensely as he glanced from side to side to gauge the reaction of the others. There was none. He took two steps toward the door and, suddenly remembering his girlfriend, asked, "Can she come?"

Natalie looked at the frail young woman. She felt a twinge of guilt at leaving her in a room of felons, but also remembered this was sometimes used as a ploy by offenders. When caught in a lie, they would tell the judge, "I would have told the probation people the truth, but my girlfriend was right there and she don't know."

"I'm sorry," Natalie apologized to the girl. "Please feel free to go get some coffee or something down the street. This will take a little over an hour."

"Oh, that's OK," she replied. Her tone seemed a mix of fear and bewilderment. "I think I should wait right here."

Natalie made a special mental note of the word 'should.' "Whatever you think is best, ma'am," she responded. She turned her attention back to her interview. "Let's get started," she said as she again motioned for him to enter the office.

Eric walked in and waited for Natalie to close the door. "I'm sorry," he apologized when he was sure he was out of hearing range of the others. "I didn't mean anything by that. I just thought..."

"Don't worry about it," Natalie interrupted. She lead the cleancut young man through the maze and to the bull pen. She didn't like leading the offenders. There was something about having them behind her, even briefly and in this controlled environment, that left her uneasy. But the complex pattern of zigs and zags made instruction from behind more trouble than it was worth. So she led with a pace that usually left them several steps behind, and an arm's length out of reach.

"Have a seat," she instructed, pointing to the empty chair on the far side of her desk. She opened the file and began the routine. "Do you know why you're here today?"

Eric thought for a moment. "I'm here for probation, I guess."

"Not exactly," she responded. "Today we're beginning your pre-sentence investigation. This is a report, about you, that we write for the judge. This will entail a series of interviews with yourself, family members, and the victim. Then we do an extensive criminal check. Once we have all the information together and verified, we make a sentencing recommendation to the court." She looked at Eric. He seemed to still be with her. "I want to make one thing very clear," she warned him. "I verify everything. So it's very important that you tell me the truth. I've yet to make a good recommendation on someone who lies to me."

"I'm not gonna lie," Eric confirmed eagerly. "I've got nothing to lie about. I swear."

Natalie decided to soften the tone. No need to start on a defensive note. "I'm sure you don't intend to lie," she stated with reassurance. "You have to understand that I give this same explanation to every person who comes in here."

Eric felt himself relax a bit. He sensed that she could tell that he wasn't like the other bums in the lobby. "I'm sorry if I sound edgy," he explained. "But I've just been through so much with this whole thing over the past couple of months."

"It's been difficult for you," Natalie reflected.

"It sure has." Eric unzipped his jacket and sat back in his chair. It was his turn to spill the well-prepared lines. "I've gotta start by tellin' ya, I've made some big mistakes over the past year. I got involved with this girl who was way too young for me. Things got carried away. Then she got scared when her mom found out."

"Then what happened?" Natalie encouraged.

"Then she changed everything," he said in a childlike, regressed voice. "She said we had intercourse. That I penetrated her. That's not true. We had oral sex three times. That's it," he emphasized. "There was no penetration."

"Did your lawyer tell you that?" Natalie asked, matter-of-factly.

"Tell me what?"

"That oral sex was not sexual penetration."

"Well, no," he answered. It hadn't occurred to him that he should discuss this new wrinkle in his story with his lawyer. He thought that admitting to doing something, just part of it, the least incriminating part, might make him sound more believable. "But,..." he continued, hesitatingly, "I mean, it's obvious. I mean..." He was looking for the right words. "I don't want to be gross," he continued sheepishly.

"Just say what's on your mind," Natalie encouraged. "I know this isn't easy. It's a delicate subject."

"OK...thanks," he said. "You're makin' this a lot easier than I thought it would be," he complimented. He paused for a moment, then remembered where he was. "It's just that...if nothing actually goes in...well...you know what I mean. It's just common sense."

"OK," Natalie responded as she turned her attention back to the file. "I didn't mean to sidetrack you."

"That's OK," he said. "I was pretty much done. I mean, I just want you to know that I know that dating someone so much younger than me shows that I have a problem. So, I'm in counseling. I go two times a month and I brought a letter from my therapist." He opened the envelope and presented the letter. "I did this on my own. I didn't do it because some court made me. I think it's important that you know that."

"Very good," Natalie said, in a complimentary tone. "Since you have that open," she said, pointing to the envelope, "what else did you bring me?"

"Everything on the list that I have," he stated eagerly. This was going better than he had dreamed. "Birth certificate, GED, my pay stub, my written version of the offense just like I told it to you, the names and addresses of all my family, my driver's license, and my social security card."

*This is too good to be true*, Natalie thought. She took the articles and examined them. "If you'll be patient for just a minute, I'll make copies of these and be right back," she said as she rose.

"Take your time," he responded as he took his jacket off and laid it over his lap.

"By the way," she said, "I noticed that you pled 'nolo contendere.'"

"What?"

"Sorry," she apologized. "All this legal mumbo jumbo gets complicated. What it boils down to is, you don't have to give a written statement if you don't want to, since you didn't plead guilty."

"Yeah, I know," he responded. "My lawyer told me I could just ignore that. But I was thinking this morning, I don't have anything to hide. I know I shouldn't have been dating a young girl like that. But it's not like I raped her or we actually…well…you know." He paused, then repeated, "I don't have anything to hide."

"Very good," Natalie said brightly. As she crossed the room with the documents, her eyes met with the amused look in those of Donna Keller, which made it immediately clear that she had listened to most of the interview. Natalie also felt that the two had the same word in mind. *Sucker!*

*Information and Belief*

*This is easier than I thought it would be,* Eric thought. He chastised himself for having gone so far into hock for a lawyer. Eric was well aware that people had always liked him. He didn't need to pay some slime in a suit to make that happen. This lady just wanted him to make it easy for herself to fill out her forms.

"Look," an intrusive, booming voice bellowed. "If you're not in the hospital or in jail, you need to be here on your report day. I've got 30 people to see today. That means I don't have time to spend on the phone with people with lame excuses." There was a pause. "Then start walking." This was immediately followed by the sound of a receiver being slammed back into the cradle.

Eric felt a sudden sense of amusement and relief. Luck of the draw had put him at this desk instead of that one. But he knew he needed more than luck. He knew to fall back on what had always worked. He scanned the desk for any clues as to who Ms. Fisher was. He began the inventory. Neat desk. No family pictures. The coffee cup had a bulldog with the initials USMC. He thought for a minute. Oh, yeah. The Marines. A diploma. Mercy College. A Catholic. He smiled when he noted that the major was social work. *This is too easy,* he concluded.

"This should go pretty quickly," Natalie assured as she returned the original documents. "It really helps when you have everything in order."

"Yes ma'am," Eric responded. "I just can't stand it when things are out of order."

As was her custom, Natalie began with the basic information sheet. She and Eric quickly shot a series of one to two-word questions and answers back and forth like a tennis volley. When she felt comfortable with the rhythm and the feel of the interview, she moved in on the key areas.

"Do you have a juvenile court record?" she asked.

Eric hesitated. "Not really."

"What does 'not really' mean?"

"Huh?"

"Well," Natalie said with a smile and a coaxing tone, "When the answer is no, people usually say so. But when there's something there…you know…something minor that you're worried someone might misunderstand, then the answer I usually get is 'not really.'"

"Well, the thing is…they have a record, but it's not of anything I did wrong."

In Natalie's head a voice yelled, *They don't keep a record of the Mayor giving you a key to the city!* "OK," she said. "What do they have on record?"

"You see," he began and sheepishly looked to the ground, "My mom and dad are alcoholics. They never let anything get in the way of their drinkin'." He paused and leaned forward, resting his elbows on his knees. His eyes remained fixated on some invisible spot on the floor in front of him. "They'd throw me out of the house if they thought a kid would bring the party down. Then, when the police would find me wandering the streets and bring me home, they'd say I ran away to cover their tracks."

"How old were you when that started?" Natalie asked empathetically.

"I can't remember a time when they didn't drink," he answered somberly. "I was walkin' off from the time I could walk."

"How long did it go on?"

"The juvie court eventually moved me to my grandma's. I guess I was about 12 then."

"So," Natalie summarized as she jotted some notes, "You left home due to neglect, were charged as a runaway several times, and you were finally placed with your grandmother."

"That's right," he agreed.

"So," Natalie concluded, "I won't find anything but status offenses."

"You shouldn't," he responded.

Natalie paused. She decided to let his choice of the word "shouldn't" go by. She felt she was doing too well to shift to an adversarial position. "OK," she said, turning to the next page of the interview booklet. "Do you have an adult criminal record?"

"Not really," he responded.

Natalie paused, set her pen down and looked squarely at the young man before her. With a slight note of amusement in her voice she said, "Didn't we just go over that whole 'not really' thing?"

Eric froze for a moment. Natalie could see the wheels turning as he searched her face for a hint of meaning. "Oh yeah," he busted out, in a tone denoting realization.

*Information and Belief*

Natalie picked up her pen. "Please list the 'not reallys,' starting with the most recent and working backward."

"No," Eric said with a laugh. "I don't have anything on LEIN!"

"It sounds like I don't have to explain the Law Enforcement Information Network to you, and that's good. But that's not what I asked," Natalie stated, attempting to withhold the impatience she was feeling from her voice.

"I just have a few traffic things," Eric replied. "Nothin' worth goin' to jail for."

"So we're talking about speeding, running stop signs...things like that?"

"Yeah, like that," he agreed.

"But no drunk driving, fleeing and eluding the police...you know, more serious stuff?"

Eric paused. "Well, you know...sometimes if you don't pull over the first second that the cops hit the lights, they try to stick it to ya," he responded defensively.

"Were you convicted on fleeing and eluding?" she asked.

"I took a plea...you know." He softened his voice in a confiding tone. "I just wanted to get it over with. They held me over the weekend. By Monday morning I would have confessed to anything if it meant I could pay a fine and leave."

"What city did that happen in?"

"Riverview," he responded. "But it's just a misdemeanor."

"Do you remember the month and year?"

"I think it was June or July of '93," he said. "But what's the big deal? You're not gonna send me to prison for driving too long after the police turn on a red light?"

"If you find yourself in prison, sir," Natalie stated flatly, "it won't be for fleeing and eluding. It will be for this case."

"But I'm not goin' to prison," Eric responded in a pleading tone. "I need to get that HYTA status." He looked at Natalie and his eyes began to well up with tears. "You don't understand. It's always been my dream to join the Marines. With this on my record, it'll never happen."

"Your considering a military career?" Natalie asked.

"I've wanted it ever since I was a kid," he continued. "You see, I was raised in a good, Catholic home by my grandmother. She used to tell me stories about her father. He was a Marine. I never got to meet him. He died in Vietnam." He rested his arm on her desk and leaned forward, lowering his voice as he continued. "He wasn't like my parents. He always took care of his kids. Even when he was away. That's because he believed in honor."

"I see," Natalie acknowledged as she scribbled some notes.

"And that's why anyone who knows me and Brenda knows that I'm tellin' the truth. Even if my parents were real losers, I spent the last few years with my grandma. We live in a nice home in a good area with good neighbors."

"Uh huh," Natalie responded, now curious where this was leading.

"You know where she lives?" he asked, but left no time for a reply. "The projects." He glanced around and smiled, as though the two were privy to an inside joke. "With you workin' here, I don't have to tell you what kind of girls live there."

Natalie took a similar glance around and returned his smile. "Tell me anyway."

"They're all lookin' for the same thing. A baby to live off of. They don't give a...well...excuse me for sayin' it...don't give a shit about a dad. As a matter of fact, that's the last thing they want around. Can't collect welfare if the baby's dad lives with ya."

"Just looking for a handout," Natalie suggested.

"You know it. But then what do I get?" he asks as he leans back, shaking his head. "I get one who don't want her momma to know that she's, she's...workin' on her future, if you know what I mean? I could name five guys she's been with since me. And that's the God's honest truth."

Natalie had heard enough. "I think I have all the basic information I need, Mr. James. You need to step back into the lobby and I'll sign you up for drug testing. You're free to go after you leave a sample. I'll be contacting your family, employer, and therapist for the report. Also, I need to verify your residence. When is the best time to come by?"

"Do I have to be home? And why do I have to be drug tested? This doesn't have anything to do with drugs."

"Actually, we could kill two birds with one stone if I could come by when your grandmother's there. That way, I could verify your family information with her at the same time. The drug test is done

*Information and Belief*

on all cases. I can't tell you how many times I've had someone tell me that their case isn't drug related, only to find out after the test that they've been using crack for years. Motive isn't always obvious."

"Do you really need to talk to her? My grandma I mean. After all, she's awfully old and I don't want this thing to upset her more than it already has."

"I appreciate your concern for her feelings, sir. I'll certainly do my best not to upset her. I just need to confirm the names, ages, and addresses of your family members, and that you live with her. It's more a formality than anything else."

"She's usually home before noon."

"So, could I call her now to set an appointment?" Natalie asked as she reached for the phone.

"I don't think she's home today. She said somethin' about goin' shoppin' before I left."

"OK," Natalie said, jotting herself a note on her desk calendar. 'Call James GM in AM.' "By the way, sir. I did have one more question before you go."

"Sure."

"Do you know a girl named Amy Mac?"

Eric felt a sudden rush to his head. His throat tightened. "Who?"

"Amy Mac," she repeated in an even tone.

Eric was silent, not knowing if he should answer. Natalie broke the silence.

"What about April Lauber. Do you know her?"

"What are you talkin' about?" Eric asked with hostility. "What do they have to do with anything?"

"It just seems, Mr. James, that you're involved in an awful lot of these kind of misunderstandings."

"I don't know who gave you those names," he snapped. "But those girls are both friends of Brenda's." Eric realized suddenly that his voice was just slightly softer than a full-fledged shout. He pulled his temper back. "Look, Ms. Fisher, I know I've made a lot of mistakes. I guess I was what you might call a player. I dated a lot. But that's all different now. I'm engaged to that girl you saw outside. My wild days are over. I'm done with girls like that." He paused. "I guess the one thing I learned was…just 'cause it's easy, don't mean it's free."

# Chapter 11

"Could you believe that guy?" Natalie laughed as she returned to the bull pen after escorting Eric to the lobby.

"I think we need to have a scientific study to determine the correlation between Catholicism and felonious behavior," Keller replied.

"Not just Catholic," Natalie continued as she lifted and displayed her coffee cup, "Catholic Marines."

"If the Pope gets word of this," Ed interjected, "We're all in trouble."

"Stop laughing," Natalie said sheepishly. "I'm ashamed to admit how many Catholic Marine wannabes I had to interview before I caught on."

"He's going to be a royal pain to supervise," Donna said in a more serious tone.

"I only caught parts of it," Ed added. "But he's not exactly your typical CSC."

Natalie thought for a moment. "How so?" she asked. "He brought everything in order…in that cute little compulsive way…he was on time, denied any responsibility for the crime and blamed the victim. That's pretty typical."

"But he was so transparent," Ed observed. He sipped his coffee and stared into the cup. Then looking up, and continued. "I can't put my finger on it. But he lacked that…smoothness."

"I know what you mean," Donna concurred. "He lacks that pillar-of-the-community quality. He kind of comes off more like a petty crook."

"That's true Ed," Natalie agreed, then turned to Donna. "I don't know that I'll be supervising him. He got hit with three counts of 3rd degree. If the judge even stays in the same ball park as the guidelines, he should be a straight incarceration recommendation."

"But I thought I heard it was a HYTA referral."

"It is," Natalie confirmed as she made her way to her ringing phone.

"A good attorney can ask for anything," Ed retorted. "Doesn't mean he'll get it." He took a bite out of his doughnut.

"If the attorney was that good, then this whole thing about him having oral sex was a new invention of his own."

"It's funny how many of 'em don't think that oral sex counts as penetration."

"And since he admitted it...in writing, no less...it scores on guidelines."

She answered the phone. "Probation...Ms. Fisher."

"Hi," greeted the familiar voice on the other end. "How's your day going?"

Natalie leaned back in her chair, taking full advantage of the quarter-inch of give that the worn spring in the back rest would allow. This effect was typical. Although it was no miracle cure, the voice of her lover was soothing and could take the edge off the most stressful day. "Typical," she answered, then added with her best Rod Serling impression, "If one works...in the Twilight Zone." The humming of the familiar theme music in the background by her coworkers was a quick reminder that this...as with all calls...was not private. "How's your day going?"

"Things are really tense around here," Gwen answered in a barely audible whisper. "You remember that meeting I was talking about for the past couple of days?" This question was rhetorical, as this was, basically, the only thing she had been talking about for the past week. She continued. "It was just what I thought. Layoffs."

"That really sucks," Natalie commiserated. "Are they at least going to wait until after Christmas?"

"It gets worse," Gwen continued in a hushed tone. "The way it times out, after the processing of the paperwork and all, it will be announced in a week and a half."

"Ouch. So that means they'll be out just, what?" Natalie pause as she glanced at her wall calendar and did a quick countdown. "Just six days before Christmas."

"And we can't leak a word of it. These guys aren't getting any warning, other than rumors, which right now they don't seem to be buying, based on the way I hear them say they're spending this year."

Natalie could hear the pain in Gwen's voice. She wasn't what Natalie considered to be the typical Human Resources Manager in a mid-sized auto plant. Natalie's vision, drawn from her brief experience in the automobile industry while working her way through college, was of the personnel manager who sat behind a desk all day. She recalled that whenever someone was sent for, that man would quickly review their file so he would know their wife's name and how many children they had. "Makes small talk easier," he would say.

But Gwen was different. She spent more time on the production floor than in her office. She made it her first task to learn the basics of every job in the plant. She felt this was the best and only way to pick the right person for a given job, and determine fairly when an employee had a problem making the production standards. She knew all 204 production employees as well as the 110 salaried employees, numbers that she considered demonstrated just how top-heavy the company was. She made it a point to know more than their names. She knew their families, their backgrounds, their hobbies. She helped them through personal crisis, and helped them find any assistance they might need.

"How do you start?" Natalie asked in a morbidly curious way. "I mean, how do you choose?"

"I really can't talk now," Gwen said. "I just wanted you to know."

"Well, I'm sorry," Natalie said sincerely. "I know this is hard on you."

"Thanks, that's really why I called."

"I know. See you tonight."

"It'll be late."

"OK, just get there when you can."

"Bye."

"Bye."

# Chapter 12

Eric and Sophia rode in silence. He seethed with anger as he recalled the large black man standing at his heels, looking over his shoulder as he urinated.

"Hi, Gran," Eric said warmly as he and Sophia entered his grandmother's home. He kissed her cheek. "What's cookin'? Smells great."

"When you called this morning and said the two of you would be stopping by, I put a roast in the oven. It should be ready any minute," she beamed.

"You didn't have to go to all that fuss," he said as he pulled a chair away from the table. "You look tired," he said with concern. "You just sit and let me check the roast."

Sophia watched the scene unfold with the same envy she always felt toward this woman. She had never seen Eric treat anyone the way he treated his grandmother.

Eric slipped an oven mitt on one hand while pushing the oven light switch on with the other. He pulled the door ajar and inhaled deeply as he gazed at the perfect care his grandmother had taken to arrange the potatoes, carrots, and celery around the meat. He loved that she always took the time to do that. He poked it with the long cooking fork and announced, "It's ready." He put on the second oven mitt and removed the dish.

"Careful," his grandmother warned. "It's very hot, dear."

"Of course it's hot," Sophia said with a playful laugh. "He just took it out of an oven."

Eric glared at her. "Don't laugh at my Gran," he snapped.

"I didn't mean anything by it," Sophia said apologetically.

"Of course you didn't," the elderly woman said as she reached to the young girl and patted her hand.

"Gran," Eric began as he pulled another chair close to her and sat, "there's something I need to talk to you about." He hesitated for a moment. "Can we do that now?" he asked softly.

"Certainly, dear," she responded as she took one of his hands in hers. She sensed that this was serious, and motioned for Sophia to take the seat on the other side of the table. "A little talk will give the dinner a chance to cool before serving."

"I'm in trouble again, Gran." His eyes welled up.

"It's OK," she comforted. "We've been through trouble before and it's always worked out."

"It's not the same," he said, his voice cracking from genuine tears. "I...I could go to prison, Gran."

The woman gasped and quickly covered her mouth with both hands. Eric looked at her, seeing her age clearly for the first time. She was slight and frail. "I'm sorry Gran...I'm so sorry," he cried. He knelt next to her, buried his head in her lap and wept uncontrollably for several minutes as she stroked his hair as a stunned Sophia watched helplessly.

The tears began to subside. "What happened?" the elderly woman asked gently.

"I swear to you, Gran," he said as he looked up, "nothin' happened the way their makin' it sound like it did."

"Slow down," she said softly, "and tell me everything."

"It happened when Sophia and I broke up," he started as he wiped his eyes on his sleeve. She handed him a tissue from the box she always kept in the kitchen. "I started dating this girl that I met through a friend. Things got serious and we...well...we had sex a few times. The next thing I know, her mother finds out and the girl says I raped her so she don't get into no trouble."

"Oh my God," she sighed.

"It gets worse. It ends up that she lied to me about how old she really was. She said she was 17."

"How old was she?" she asked tentatively.

"Thirteen," he whispered.

Her eyes widened. "She was just a child," she said with disbelief.

"I swear I didn't know," he pleaded. "If you saw her, you'd understand. She doesn't look like she's 13."

"I've seen her," Sophia added. Eric and his grandmother seemed startled, as they has forgotten she was in the room. Sophia continued. "She looks older than I do."

Gran resisted making the observation that Sophia didn't look much older herself, and instead, returned her attention to her grandson. "What will happen now?"

"I already pled guilty. My lawyer said because of her age, it didn't matter if she said yes or not."

"But surely the judge would understand if she lied and she looks older," she said.

"She's going to lie to him, just like she lied to her mom and the cops. My lawyer says the prosecutor will have her dress like a little girl. Then if she gets up in front of the judge, lookin' like that and makin' me sound like an animal, I could go away forever."

"It doesn't make sense," the elderly woman said indignantly. "Isn't there anyone we can talk to?"

"Well Gran, that's where we're at now. This woman is going to do a report for the judge. She's gonna be comin' around and askin' a lot of questions. I...I told her I still live here."

"What?" she said with astonishment. "Why did you do that? It's not against the law to live with your girlfriend."

"Well...on my way over there, I was thinkin'. Remember when I first told you I was gonna move in with Sophia?"

She nodded.

"You didn't like it. You thought it was wrong to live with her before we got married."

"I'm sorry," she said firmly, "That's just the way I was brought up."

"Right," he said emphatically. "And what if that lady was brought up that way, too? She probably already thinks I'm a sex addict. The cops have been tellin' her stuff, too. You know how they feel about me here."

"They've always seemed to have it in for you," his grandmother agreed.

He took both of her hands into his. "I need your help. I know how you feel about people who lie. I can't believe I..." he started to tear up again. "I made it so you'd have to lie. If I'd of thought about it longer before I started talkin' I wouldn't of done it. But I remembered that look on your face when you said I was movin' in with Sophia and..."

"It's OK," she reassured. "It isn't exactly a lie. Sometimes, you still get mail here. In my heart, you'll always be with me."

Eric's head returned to her lap, where he continued to cry.

# Chapter 13

Natalie searched the index in the back of the Downriver Road Atlas. Cavin Ave. Page 84, D-6. She shook her head in self-beratement after jogging her memory with the visual aid of the map. She had been there a week and a half ago. She knew it was two blocks off the main road. But was that Middlebelt or Merriman? She always got those two mixed up. "Middlebelt," she mumbled.

"What?" Donna asked as she pulled her purse from the lower desk drawer.

"Just babbling," Natalie responded.

"You riding the desk all day?"

"No, just planning the route. What about you? Are you headed for the field or just a quick smoke break?"

"I'm going downtown for the court computer and..." Donna paused for effect, and lowering the tone of her voice added, "the dreaded write-up room."

"If we never see you again, I'll tell your parents you love them," Natalie said with a laugh.

"Where are you off to?"

"You remember that out-of-county transfer request I was talking about last week?"

"Which one?"

Natalie was momentarily annoyed by her own ridiculous question. The two women likely discussed 20 cases a week. She knew she needed to be more specific. "Sorry. It's the *You've come a long way, baby* case." Natalie smiled as a look of confusion was quickly followed by wide-eyed recognition.

Natalie recalled the day she had given this case its tag name. "This case," she had explained in front of the usual bull pen audience of Bradner, Keller, and Green, "brings a new feminine hero to our ranks. As statistics have shown," she explained in a studious tone, "women are the true underachievers of the criminal justice system. If you've got a woman on your caseload, it's a 95 percent certainty that she committed a property crime. Am I right?" After acknowledging their nods of agreement, she continued. "According to this transfer report, this lady was convicted of car jacking and assault and battery.

*Information and Belief*

And," she added while producing the conviction and referral slip, "the A & B was pled down from Felonious Assault."

"So, she darn near killed somebody," Bradner concluded.

"It gets better," Natalie continued. "This is her third felony."

"Wow," Donna said with a chuckle.

"Wait," Natalie continued. "That's not the topper." She paused for affect. "Just to blow the stats right out the window...she's 64 years old."

"No!" Donna's chuckle quickly reverted into a gasp.

"Atta girl," Bradner said as he pantomimed a toast.

"You've come a long way baby," Natalie added.

Donna's statement returned her to the present conversation. "I thought you made the home call on that last week when you stopped at Westland PD for me."

"I did. A week and a half ago," she corrected. "Time flies when you're having fun."

"Then why the return visit?"

"She didn't come in," Natalie responded. "I had her scheduled for yesterday morning."

"Imagine," Keller said, feigning astonishment. "An unreliable felon."

"Go figure," Natalie laughed as she quickly organized her desk and tucked the file into her bag.

Her phone rang as she put her jacket on. Her eyes darted from it to the answering machine and back.

"Don't do it," Keller warned.

"It'll just be there tomorrow," Natalie said with resignation.

"Your funeral," Keller laughed. "I'm outta here." She waved as she exited, leaving Natalie alone in the room for the first time that day.

"Probation, Ms. Fisher," she announced into the phone.

"Ahhh, hi. Can I talk to Ms. Fisher?" the unsteady caller asked.

*Lucky its me*, she thought, recalling Mr. Moore's response to the last caller who ignored his opening identification.

"You're not going to believe this," Moore had said indignantly as he had stormed into the bull pen. The outburst didn't alarm them, as they were used to Moore's tirades. "You've got to come with me. 'Cause if you don't see the stupidity, your not going to believe it."

"That's a challenge I can't resist," Bradner said as he and the others followed the senior agent back to his office.

"As you can see," Moore had started, pointing to his phone, "I have someone on hold. Now, just listen to this." He snapped up the receiver. "Probation, Moore here," he announced. After listening for a few seconds, he bellowed, "Hold on, I'll go look for him." He punched the hold button and dropped the receiver to his desk. "Can you believe this burnout?"

"I don't get it," Keller responded softly.

"This is the fifth time I've answered this call, "Probation, Moore here," and this is the fifth time this crackhead has said, "Uh...uh...yeah. Is Mr. Moore in?"

The group laughed.

"So let's just start an office pool, shall we?" he continued. "How many times do I have to answer the phone like this before this jerk figures it out?"

"But Mr. Moore," Bradner said, mimicking the same voice Moore had used when impersonating the caller, "When you carry the crack pipe in your ears, it leaves your pockets free."

"No doubt," Moore replied with a laugh. He looked at the receiver with resignation. "I guess I better let young Mr. Einstein in on the punch line. I've got other things to do." He reached for the receiver and mumbled, "I hope this clown doesn't have kids. Some gene pools just shouldn't go forward."

"Remember, he's the future of this fine country of ours," Natalie baited.

"I've heard Canada is lovely this time of year," Bradner said as the group disbanded.

"Probation, Moore here."

*Stay focused*, Natalie chastised herself as she returned her attention to her caller. "This is Ms. Fisher."

"This is Ed Miller. How are you?"

"I'm fine, and you?"

"Things have been better," he began. "I'm supposed to be in tomorrow."

*Information and Belief*

"That's right Mr. Miller. If you're not dead or in jail on another charge, you should be here tomorrow. Those are the only excuses the department acknowledges," she responded quickly, hoping to head off one of his many endless excuses.

"Oh, its not that. I'll be in," he assured. "The thing is, its awfully close to Christmas."

*And you'd better hope Santa's given up on that whole obsessive hobby of tracking who's been naughty and nice,* she thought.

"Anyway," he continued, "It's my kids. I know I'm supposed to come with a restitution payment tomorrow. And I'm not asking for myself," he added hastily, "but they're going to really suffer if I have to shell out $510 again this month. So, I figured, the money's just going to some big company anyway and what's the harm in…"

"Mr. Miller," Natalie interrupted. "As I recall from having done your background investigation, you haven't seen your son since a few months after he was born."

"Yeah, but since then…"

"Let me finish," Natalie continued with exasperation. "Also, as I recall, your theft was discovered just before Christmas last year. The two owners of the company had to use their credit cards to make their house payments, and had to let seven people go because they couldn't make payroll."

"Look," he replied angrily, "I didn't take half as much as they said I did. They doctored those books to get rich off my mistake."

"First of all, sir, it was a theft, not a mistake. Secondly, they sent me copies of every check and credit card receipt you signed…"

"Yeah, but they…"

"And finally, I don't intend to retry your case here today." Natalie glanced at her watch and winced. She had wanted to be on the road a half hour ago. "Bring your payment, sir."

"Do you have kids, Ms. Fisher?" he whined.

*Nice try,* she thought before saying, "We're not here to talk about me, sir. Just come in tomorrow with your payment."

"I'll see you tomorrow," he said, sounding resigned to his fate.

As the conversation concluded, Ms. Green led another probationer past her desk.

"I don't care what they say," she was saying angrily. "Its 4 p.m. and the lobby's packed with people. I don't have to put up with this mess. I've got a class to get ready for. I'm not seein' anybody past 4:30. Anyone here after that will just have to come back at 8 a.m. on my office day."

Natalie glanced back and her eyes met those of the nameless recipient. His mixed expression of confusion and astonishment told her that they shared the same thought. Natalie quickly gathered her things and bolted from the office. She didn't want to be around to hear the angry shouts and groans from the lobby when Ms. Green announced that she was single-handedly changing the Michigan Department of Corrections office report hours.

# Chapter 14

The sun was already beginning to set as Natalie left the office. The clouds that had dominated the skyline for the majority of the day had given way just in time to create a blinding westward commute. Still, a glimpse of the sun during the short days of a Michigan winter was an appreciated change for Natalie. She kept her eyes on the road as she squirmed and fiddled with her seatbelt. Its clasp pushed against the bulge created by her gun. She knew that many agents went with the shoulder holster for just that reason. But she didn't like wearing it when she would be spending the better part of the day in the office, since, by policy, all weapons had to be concealed at all times. She would have had to wear a blazer all day. A mandatory blazer could turn in to a torture device in an office without decent temperature regulation. Add that to the day-long smell of sweaty leather, the pulling and squeaking sound that can be easily heard in a quiet room, and the stain that it leaves on your blouse. On the other hand, on a mild winter or fall day, it was the perfect holster for under a light jacket. "A girl's got to accessorize," she once told Gwen playfully, when explaining the need for three holsters and one gun.

She switched the heat down three notches as she made a right turn off Van Born to Middlebelt Road. The fact that the address was in Westland had added to her confusion. Until double-checking her map, she hadn't realized that any part of Westland would be that far south. But the map had confirmed the address. Westland was a city that engulfed its neighbors. It somehow managed to border Inkster and Garden City on three sides.

She took a left down the side street. This particular little strip was located just south of Inkster. The neighborhood was quiet and lined with mature trees. Natalie spotted the little brick ranch she had visited previously, and slowed to scan the street. An elderly man three houses down was salting his walk. With no other sign of life evident, she gave herself the go-ahead to stop on the first pass. If anything had looked out of place, she would have driven around the block for a second look.

She fell into her usual routine. Park on the street, not in the driveway, don't want to trap yourself with only one way out, if possible. She left the car unlocked; better to lose a stereo than have to fumble with keys while trying to make a fast retreat. She checked the sides as she approached the house. Next were the window curtains for movement, and then the pause, to listen for dogs.

Confident that she had covered her bases, she knocked on the door, making certain to stand slightly sideways, her strong side away from the door. She felt her body tense up as the deep bark of a dog intensified her state of mental readiness. She heard footsteps and noticed the curtain of the bay window move. Then, a few more slow footstep and the door was open.

She saw before her a man who looked to be in his early 70s. His once-blue eyes were covered in white, milky cataracts. He held the large yellow dog back by the collar with one hand while supporting himself with a cane held in the other. His build was slight, and he appeared to be about one inch shorter than Natalie. He smiled, displaying a prominent broken front tooth. "Can I help you?" he asked in a soft, sincere voice.

"Yes, sir," Natalie responded politely. "My name is Ms. Fisher and I'm with the Probation Department. I left a letter here the other day for a Ms. Tucker. Does she live here, sir?"

"Yes, she does," he answered kindly. "I found that letter on the door and gave it to her." He released the dog, snapped his fingers and pointed toward the left corner of the house. The animal obediently walked away. "Won't you come in?" he invited, opening the storm door.

His frail appearance and gentle nature put her a bit more at ease. "Is Ms. Tucker in, sir?" she asked again.

"Yes, please come in, dear," he said again, opening the door a bit wider. A sudden gust of wind pulled him off balance, and he was straining.

Natalie grabbed the door. "I've got it," she assured him. She stepped into the foray and glanced to the left. The dog was sitting quietly in the corner.

"I guess I'm a little old to be fighting Mother Nature," he said jokingly.

"Aren't we all," Natalie agreed, returning his smile.

"Have a seat, dear. I'll just turn the TV down." He turned and slowly hobbled toward the set.

Natalie remained standing by the entrance and glanced around him at the screen. In most homes, at this hour, she'd be catching the closing of the Opra show. She did a double take, certain that her eyes, obviously in a state of malfunction, had registered incorrectly. The screen was filled with the full-color view of one woman engaging another in oral sex. Next to them, a man was masturbating and giving them instructions. "Yeah, baby. Do her with your fingers, too."

The old man snapped the set off, turned, and smiled. Natalie looked at the cataract-covered eyes, and her first thought was, *My God, mom was right. Too much of that will make you go blind.* Then she surveyed the room. She spotted a Hustler magazine on the end table, and the empty film case, along with a few others, on the floor by the television. An open magazine, displaying a woman spread-eagled and masturbating, lay on the coffee table.

Natalie's momentary amusement turned into panic. She hadn't checked behind the door or casually pushed it until it met the wall, to assure that there was no one behind it as she entered. Her back felt suddenly vulnerable. She casually stepped the needed half-pace toward the door without turning her back on the man. She tried to make it look more like a nonchalant shift of weight than a step. She let her elbow hit the heavy wooden door and felt her heart returning to its normal pace when she heard the reassuring sound of the doorknob tap against the wall.

She returned her focus to the old man, who continued to smile at her. She had the distinct feeling that he got some kind of strange kick out of the fact that she had seen what he was watching on TV.

Natalie felt like a pawn in someone else's sick little game, and she didn't like it. "Is Ms. Tucker in, sir?" she asked sternly.

"She's in Bay City," he replied as he tottered back toward her. "She won't be back until about 10 this evening.

"I thought you said she was here when you let me in, sir," Natalie said in a confrontational tone.

"Oh," he replied innocently, a look of concern crossing his face. "I thought you asked if she lives here. Not, is she here now. But," he added with a smile, "You can stay and wait for her if you want."

"Look," Natalie said impatiently, "please tell her that I was here, and that if I don't hear from her by 12 noon tomorrow, I'll deny the transfer and recommend a warrant for violation of probation." She pulled a card from her badge case and dropped it on the coffee table just to the left of the magazine.

Natalie turned and reached for the storm door handle. She heard a sudden rustling, then her arm was being pulled down by the sleeve of her jacket.

The dog's fangs had sunk into the thick sleeve of her winter coat. She gave one quick yank. The animal, snarling, still had her. When he released slightly and lunged to get a better grip, Natalie pulled again. Her arm was free. She pushed the storm door open, quickly stepped to the other side, and closed it, smacking the diligent animal on the nose as it mounted another attack.

"Bad dog," she heard the old man say as she, now safely on the other side of the door, checked her wrist and coat for damage. She noted the lack of sincerity or surprise in his tone.

# Chapter 15

"Hi." Gwen's voice cheerfully greeted Natalie as she pulled her boots off on the slippery linoleum of the entry way. She re-examined the sleeve of her long, bulky coat before hanging it in the closet. Not a mark.

Natalie turned to look at her lover. Tall and slender, with light blond hair and blue eyes, sporting feminine attire as usual, with tasteful makeup. Gwen could easily pass for straight.

"So," she began, "you won't believe what's going on. It started this morning with…"

"Yeah, yeah," Natalie interrupted. "Loss of jobs, end of livelihood, chaos, lives devastated. Yada, yada. Now, let's talk about *me*."

Gwen looked startled for a moment. Then she saw the mischievous grin on Natalie's face and the two burst into laughter. "It must have been one hell of a day," Gwen concluded.

Natalie relayed the incident with the old man, up to the point of the dog attack. "Then," she announced, "You saved my skin."

"Me?" Gwen asked suspiciously, feeling she was being set up for a punch line.

"No, really. You," Natalie assured. "Do you remember when we went shopping for my winter coat? You talked me into getting that long, goosedown coat."

"How could I forget," she responded in exasperation. "You've done nothing but whine ever since."

"You do have to admit," Natalie teased, "I'm so short and its sooo long and fluffy. I do bear a striking resemblance to Sam Kinison."

"You do not," Gwen said defensively. "Your problem is, you have a poor body image."

"Well anyway, while I was trying to leave, this dog, who looked a lot like Ol' Yeller, jumps up and latches onto my coat."

Gwen gasped.

"He would have torn the heck out of my wrist if it weren't for that damn coat."

"You see," Gwen said triumphantly. "I guess you'll take my fashion advice a bit more seriously now."

"I guess so," Natalie conceded. She flopped on the far end of the couch and put her legs up and over on Gwen as she lay her head on the overstuffed arm. "OK," she said with a laugh. "I guess I'm ready to hear about the toil and misery of others now. I'm such a self-centered pig."

"Feel free to interrupt any story I'm telling if the final point is to prove to me just how right I was," Gwen laughed, rubbing Natalie's leg. "OK, let's see if I can get my train of thought back. Oh yeah. I got in this morning and I knew something was up right away. Mr. Tocars' car was already in the lot, and he never gets there before 9:30."

"Exercising owner's privilege, no doubt."

"At every opportunity," Gwen agreed. "Only peons like me show up at 8. Anyway, they call the meeting and sure enough, layoffs."

"How many?" Natalie inquired sympathetically.

"I'm not sure. Its not that easy. Now, everyone's arguing about how we'll do it. What we have is a dollar amount that we need to cut. Some people want to lay off by department, some by classification."

"Don't you have to go by seniority?"

"We're not a union shop."

"But you usually do it that way, don't you? Isn't that part of the way to keep a union out? To give the employees the same protections that they would get without paying dues?"

"Right," Gwen agreed. "But this situation is exactly why we do that. If we can help the company survive in the long run by laying off based on ability, or by classification or by department, then we can do that."

"So, which way looks best to you?"

"It's going to hurt no matter how we do it. Business has been so good, these people had no way of knowing that Ford would bow out of its contract and buy their lock subassembly from a Mexican firm."

"I don't get it," Natalie said angrily. "I mean, isn't that why they call it a contract? Don't they have to buy your parts for as long as the contract lasts?"

"They're the Ford Motor Company. They have more lawyers on staff than we have employees. Companies know when they sign a contract with Ford that it's basically a one-way deal."

"Then why do they set themselves up like that?"

"Because they pay big."

"Like being a mistress to a millionaire," Natalie analogized.

"A very insecure mistress." Gwen laughed. "If this millionaire could get a woman who's a little less beautiful but would live in a smaller apartment and take smaller diamonds, she's out." She sighed. "I guess the point is, there is no real security in life."

Natalie laughed. "I know. I had a mangy yellow dog try to explain that to me just today. But what you're telling me sounds so familiar. Factory work sucks. I remember when my dad got promoted to plant superintendent. They had this big inspection coming up. We didn't see him at home for weeks. This damn thing was his only focus. By the time of the inspection, he'd worked something like 20 hours straight. You could have eaten off the floors in that place. He had all the numbers and charts and whatever else these kind of people look for, all organized and laid out for 'em."

"So, what happened?"

"They did the whole walk-through. Then they chewed his ass in front of everyone because, apparently, while he was working non-stop inside, it had started to rain outside. One of them decided that he had forever tainted the company image by letting the American flag fly in the rain." Natalie laughed. "He said it was the worst day of his life. He didn't even know whose job it was to raise or lower the flag. His nose hadn't been out of that shop in 20 hours, he'd completely ignored his family for weeks, and they tore his ass up because the flag was flying in the rain."

"What'd he do?"

"This is the part that always got me. He said he listened until they were finished, told someone to go take the flag down, and then went right on with the tour. I told him I would have quit. He laughed and said that not only did he not quit, he worked there long enough to watch all of those guys go down in flames."

"Really."

"Yeah. He said what I needed to learn is that you have to just keep going on. Keep doing what you know is right. Things may change slow, but they always change. It's inevitable. He also said that he wasn't doing his job for 'the flag guys.' He felt a responsibility to 'his people,' like the guys who work for him. He said he knew his real job was to keep them working. 'His people' were the folks who buy cars, too. He needed to make a safe product for them, that would last. And most of all, he said 'his people' were his family. He knew he was doing a good job for the people who really mattered. He said the trick to survival was knowing who your people are, putting them first, and understanding that you have to work through the setbacks."

"That's rather simplistic," Gwen responded defensively. "I consider the employees to be 'my people' too, but I'm out of there if I say a word. I see people extending themselves to the limit financially, and I'm supposed to stand by and smile."

Natalie was hurt that the wisdom it took her father a lifetime to acquire was so easily dismissed. But, considering the circumstances, she decided to let it go. "What are they afraid of? Sabotage, maybe?"

"That might be a part of it. People who know they're going to lose their jobs in a few weeks can get pretty angry."

"What else?"

"I think the biggest part of the secrecy is the Christmas party next week. Tocars doesn't want to get confronted by an angry group of soon-to-be unemployed workers and spouses."

"Of course not," Natalie chuckled. "That will be your job, the week after."

"Exactly," she agreed. "Heaven forbid he do his own dirty work."

"It seems like a good place to start the cuts might be with getting rid of a lavish Christmas party," Natalie suggested.

"Thanks for the advice, Ebanezor." She smirked. "Actually, someone did mention that. But Tocars was having none of it. And I quote, 'There has been a Christmas party every year for as long as we've had a company.'"

"Hey! Wait just a minute!" Natalie interjected. "Excuse me for being a little bit slow. But I just got that."

"Got what?"

"Unemployed workers and their *spouses*," she responded, with emphasis on the last word. "You didn't mention that before."

"And?" Gwen responded. "Your point is, what?"

"My point is," Natalie said in a playful tone, batting her eyes, "Whatever will I wear on such short notice?"

"Yeah, right," Gwen said grudgingly. She lifted Natalie's legs, slid her way out from under them, and dropped them back on the couch. "I don't really want to suddenly be slated as one of the people who has to go to cut expenses."

Natalie could tell by the way Gwen slapped her briefcase on the table before opening it, not quite a slam but clearly intended to end the conversation, that Gwen had seen through her patented, 'Make it sound like a joke when you're not really joking' tactic.

"I've got to go over some numbers tonight to give them an idea of what the various options would mean financially and…"

"I'm sorry," Natalie sighed.

"It's not your fault," she replied quietly.

"I know," Natalie said, taking the files from Gwen's hands and holding them gently. "But I'm sorry anyway."

"This is Detroit, not San Francisco."

"You've got to admit, it's kind of funny," Natalie said, attempting to brighten her mood. "Today I had to deal with a rapist and a voyeur. You work for a guy who would rather lay somebody off than not have a big party. Those are the people who are judging us."

"I'm not laughing," Gwen replied gloomily.

# Chapter 16

The roads were, for the most part, dry and clear, making Natalie's commute uneventful. The sky was clear, too, which led to a dramatic drop in temperature. She felt the cold bite every inch of unprotected skin on her face as she clumsily punched at the small numbered buttons with fingers made oversized by gloves. "Damn," she mumbled as she pulled the glove from her right hand and subjected her tender fingertips to the unique feel of icy cold metal.

Once inside, she made a beeline for the bull pen. She was early on a Friday morning. Most government workers tended to consider this the unofficial beginning of the weekend. The pace slows, and business tends to start at 20 minutes past the hour and conclude at 20 till the traditional end.

But for Natalie and most of the other occupants of the bull pen, this was the most hectic day of the week. Report day. Natalie always likened it, in consideration of her Catholic upbringing, to the duties of a priest. The ritualistic repetition of phrases in the blessing before the communion. "He broke the bread, gave it to his disciples and said, Take this all of you and eat it, it is my body..." But, in her case, the ritual started with, "Any police contacts or changes?" Followed by, "Did you bring your pay stub?" Upon occasion, she even got to hear a confession or two.

As she passed the row of offices, she recalled once having seen a probationer for an absent agent. The woman had smiled toward the end of the report and stated politely, "I hope you don't think it rude that I've rushed my answers. But you see, I have a good-looking man handcuffed to the bed at home, and since I had to wait in the lobby a lot longer that I expected, he's probably quit uncomfortable by now."

Natalie recalled looking at the woman. Her tone had seemed consistent with someone explaining that they were double parked. "Are you telling me that you have someone abducted and tied up at your house, ma'am?"

"Oh no," the woman had replied, seemingly hurt by the implication. "He's my boyfriend and he likes it when I do that, and then we..."

"Wohoo, hold up right there," Natalie said sternly. "That's way too much information. You keep that stuff between him and you. There's no place for that here."

The woman released a childish giggle. "I didn't mean nothin' by it. My boyfriend and I…"

"Enough!" Natalie had interrupted. Although inwardly amused, she maintained an expressionless demeanor. One of the first lessons for any agent in training is to beware of the probationer who wants to forge a special kind of relationship with you. It's a classic setup, and it needs to be shut down right away. "This isn't some game," she told the woman. "The next time I hear talk like that, I'll call the police, have them let him loose, and let the two of you explain your sex life to the judge."

But, unlike her Catholic tradition, Natalie seldom heard a "Mea culpa" uttered by the felon upon departure.

Natalie flipped the switch, illuminating the bull pen. She detected movement toward the back of the room. A small brown mouse scurried along the wall and behind the perpetually underutilized desk of Mrs. Carter. As far as Natalie was concerned, Mrs. Carter was nothing more than a legend. The headless horseman of the civil service. The rumor was that she has been on medical leave for various ailments since 1989. It was said that she popped in about once a year, worked for as long as she could without having to actually turn in anything, then, coincidentally, the day the first reports were due, had a tragic relapse. One such "Carter sighting" had occurred three months earlier. Although Natalie had been on vacation and thus not able to bear witness to the event, she was left with several sloppy, half-written, overdue reports upon her return, as evidence of the event.

"Good morning," Daniel Wood said cheerily. A handsome 35-year-old black man with short brown hair and brown eyes, some considered him a Denzel-Washington lookalike.

"Good morning," Natalie returned warmly. "How was your trip?"

"Too short," he responded with a laugh.

"Aren't they all," Natalie agreed as she reached to the back of her computer and flipped the switch.

"Hey," Henry Crew grumbled as he rushed to his desk.

"And there's another one," Natalie jested. "The prodigal son's return."

"Return?" Crew asked, running his fingers through his short, neatly cut brown hair. "Oh, that's right," he said, as though he had gotten a verbal response to the question. "Where was it you went again?"

"Down to Arkansas to see mama," Wood replied. He grimaced slightly, angry that he had let the word "mama" come out of his mouth instead of "mother." He had worked for years to sound like a successful U of M graduate instead of a poor black kid from the south. "Crew, I didn't remember you talking about annual leave before I left."

"No such luck," Crew said glumly. "The boy was sick with a fever for the past few days."

"Oh, no," Natalie said sympathetically. "What's wrong with the little guy?"

"An ear infection, I guess. Whatever it is, the key symptom is that he has to throw up on his father every hour."

Natalie and Wood laughed. "Take two aspirin and barf on dad in the morning," Wood elaborated.

"That's pretty much it," Crew agreed.

"What's pretty much it?" Bradner asked, walking in as the last words were spoken.

"Babies. They use their fathers as barf bags," Crew reiterated.

"Don't say that," Bradner whined. "You know mine is due any day now. You could at least leave me with my illusions for at least the first few days of fatherhood."

"You're better men than I," Wood said, as though reciting poetry, as he left the room.

"It'll be his turn some day," Crew said with a smile, motioning toward the path that Wood had blazed moments before.

"I don't know," Bradner said thoughtfully. "It seems like he considers everything he does to be a reflection on his people. Like, if he wasn't the perfect father, he'd be letting his people down. I sure couldn't live up to that pressure."

"Well, I haven't been a father long," Crew said, "but I can tell you one thing. Black or white, there is no such thing as the perfect parent."

Natalie smiled at the 6-foot, 3-inch, 200 pound man. On a bar night months ago, Crew had shared with her his most guarded secret – he had worked briefly as a model. He was well aware that if anyone in the world of corrections found out, he'd be mocked about it for his entire career, but he trusted Natalie enough to tell her. He always dressed in stylish suits, yet what Natalie found most attractive about him was his engaging smile. And the fact that he was one of the few truly handsome men she knew who didn't seem to judge people on their appearance.

"Fisher." Kay Elds called from the doorway, motioning for Natalie to follow. From there, she was led down the series of halls, passing most of the office's 35 agents, before entering Elds' office. Elds closed the door behind them.

"I know I've been acting kind of weird lately," she started.

Natalie sensed that the opening statement was the beginning of a long story, and decided to take a seat. Elds followed suit.

"I know it's been a real pain in the ass," she said apologetically. "Being low on the totem pole, you've been stung more than anyone. And now...well...it looks like it's going to get a little bit worse before it gets better."

Natalie's mind raced. She had grown fond of the senior agent who had taken her under her wing almost a year ago. This serious tone was new to her. Elds was one of the people who had taught Natalie the need for, and the fine art of, office banter. "OK, you've built the suspense," Natalie said in a joking manner to cover her concern. "Spill it."

"It looks like I might get suspended for a few days," she said somberly.

"What?" Natalie was shocked. Elders had a reputation for speaking her mind, but she was also considered the 'go to' person in the office. So the supervisors usually overlooked statements that would be considered insubordinate if uttered by others. "You must have pissed off someone mighty important."

"In a manner of speaking. Look, I'm not tellin' a whole lot of people right now, so I hope you'll keep it under wraps for awhile."

"Hey, no problem. I'll wait 'til you give me the green light, but what happened?"

"It's the stupidest damn thing," she began. "On second thought, maybe I'm the stupidest damn thing. The department has changed a lot over the last 10 years. I've tried to change with it. We went from law enforcer to social worker. Then from social worker to bureaucrat. Today, we just document. It doesn't matter what people do as long as we write it down." She smiled and picked up her pen. "Careful, careful!" she warned, "I have a pen and I'm not afraid to use it!"

Natalie laughed and felt comforted by the return of the old Elds.

"Anyway," Kay continued, "it's so stupid. I guess I got stuck in social worker mode. That's my degree, after all. They knew that when they hired me." She opened her desk, withdrew a business card, and handed it to Natalie. "This is what did it."

Natalie examined the card. "Wilson's Auto Repair," she read aloud. "I don't get it."

"I've got this young guy on my caseload," Kay explained. "I'm pretty sure I've told you about him before. Its a Negligent Homicide. He was driving his kid brother to school when the hots fell from his smoke. He leans over for a second to brush them off his lap and he looks up just in time to see the old woman crossing the street."

"Oh yeah," Natalie recalled. "That's a sad case."

"Yeah," she said, nodding in agreement. "A momentary lapse can ruin a lot of lives. The old woman is dead and he's wracked with guilt." She took the card from Natalie and looked at it. "Anyway. That's Wilson. So, after two years on probation and a lot of counseling, he starts to return to the living, so to speak, and he starts this business. He comes in the office, all excited, and he plops about 30 business cards on my desk."

"So?" Natalie responded.

"So, I know it's not like this guy's some crazed killer or drug dealer or something, so I handed out a few of the cards to friends. I even got my oil changed there myself. And, of course, I paid full price. Its not like I'm out there exploiting my relationship with probationers."

"And?" Natalie asked expectantly.

"There is no 'and,'" Elders said, throwing her hands up. "I'm not sure what happened from there. But management got wind of it. I don't know if someone saw me there, or if someone I gave a card to got pissed off for some reason. But I got called on the carpet."

"I still don't get it."

"Apparently, there's a violation of work rules there somewhere," Kay said with disgust. "On the other hand, fuck 'em. If they want to give me a few days off for something like that after 10 years, then there's only one thing left to do."

"What's that?" Natalie asked.

"I'm goin' to Disney World!!" she said with a wide grin as she snatched up the phone. "They think they can get me with a few lousy days off without pay. It's chump change."

Natalie laughed. "Don't you have to win the Super Bowl or something like that to go there?"

"My only regret is that I don't have a probationer who's a travel agent to throw the business to. Fuck 'em."

This made Natalie laugh even harder as she rose to her feet.

"Stop your laughing, you're the one who's going to be seeing my probationers when I'm gone and...Oh, hello," she said, turning her attention to the telephone as she gave Natalie a dismissing wave and a wink.

# Chapter 17

Natalie returned to the bull pen and found Bradner, Crew, Keller, and Wood were still milling about.

"Fisher! Moore! You two come over here. You've got to hear this," Bradner said.

Natalie turned, finding that she was less than three feet from Agent Moore, who leaned against the wall in the hallway outside of his office, leafing through the morning paper. Always ready to be filled in on the latest, he quickly diverted his attention from the entertainment section and followed Natalie.

"Go on, tell 'um," he said to an outwardly agitated Keller. "This is classic Judge Henman stuff," he added eagerly.

Keller started with a heavy sigh. "Well, about seven months ago I get this guy on my caseload. He's on for assault and battery pled down from felonious assault. I did the pre. He beat his girlfriend, almost to death, but you know how Judge Henman is on domestic violence. So he gets the plea, but the judge puts a laundry list of conditions on his probation. Batterer's counseling, AA meetings, seek/maintain employment and, of course, no contact with the victim."

"Owwww," Natalie said mockingly.

"Yeah," Moore agreed. "Why didn't he just double-dog-dare him to kill her. It'd do just as much good."

"No, wait," Keller said. "It gets better. Then, I get this guy on my caseload. Month after month I hound him, 'You've got to get into the counseling program. You've got to go to your AA meetings. You've got to get a job.' Then he says to me, 'I can't get a job. It's all I can do to keep an eye on that no good two-timin' bitch who started all this.'"

"Oh my God," Bradner laughed.

"So, I tell him," Keller continues in a stern voice, "'You've been on probation seven months and managed to do everything you weren't supposed to do and none of what you needed to do. You're goin' back in front of the judge.' Then I give him the usual speech about turning himself in when the warrant letter comes to him."

"What'd he say?" Moore asked.

*Information and Belief*

"Not much," she replied.

"So, what happened?" Natalie asked.

"This morning, I get his file back with a new order of probation."

"And?" Crew encouraged.

"The judge continued him on probation," Keller paused for effect. "And removed all the conditions."

"Ohhhhh," the group moaned collectively.

"So," Keller asks the group angrily, "How the hell do I supervise him now?"

"Yeah," Bradner commiserated. "Now he's not worried about violating his probation. He knows nothing's going to happen."

"Violate?!" Crew interjected. "How's he going to violate when he has no conditions?! Basically, the court just told him that he's required to do no more than show up one time a month for the next year."

"And if he doesn't, you can violate his probation and have the judge take that requirement away too," Natalie added. "Don't worry son," she said in a deep, majestic voice. "If you can't make it over the hurdle, we'll just lower the bar."

"That's nothin'" Moore retorted. "Back when I was an eager young agent..."

"You were once an eager young agent?" Bradner teased.

"Of course, and I'll have you know, I'm very deeply hurt by any inference to the contrary," he said, racing through the statement in a monotone fashion, causing everyone to conclude that he wasn't the least bit offended. "Anyway, it was six years ago. I was a fresh, eager young crime fighter. I had this punk come in and tell me he got arrested for assault and battery. So, the policy was the same then as it is now. It's a misdemeanor, so I send an arrest notice to, none other than our favorite Judge Ash..."

"Ohhhhh," the group moaned.

"No," he continued. "Its not what you're thinking. I recommended a warrant since it's a violent crime, and he sent the arrest notice back with the statement, 'Prepare a warrant immediately!' So I'm feelin' good. I'm feelin' like a key part of the justice system. I call the guy, tell him he's in big trouble now. He needs to get ready to see the judge. Then I write the most eloquent warrant request you've ever seen. I mean, I really put my mind to it.

It was a thing of beauty. Then," he paused, "I get the sucker back three days later. 'Warrant Denied.'"

"What?" Crew asked incredulously. "You mean he denied the warrant after he told you to write it?"

"Yep," Moore replied, putting his hands in his pockets and rocking from heel to toe. "Needless to say, calling that probationer and telling him to come in here instead of going back to court was one awkward conversation." He pantomimed a telephone using his right thumb and pinkie fingers. "Hello, Mr. Smith. Just forget about that whole warrant-for-your-arrest thing."

"The only part of that story that surprises me," Bradner said, "is that Judge Ash even bothered to respond to your arrest notice. I'll bet you anything his CAPO checked off the warrant box and sent it back."

"A Court Appointed Probation Officer isn't supposed to do that, are they?" Natalie asked.

"They do a lot of the grunt work the judges don't want to do. I've got a friend from training who had to work in Ash's courtroom for two months while his regular CAPO was on maternity leave. He said that Ash had him reading and signing arrest notices and amended orders."

Natalie rubbed her temples. "Please don't say that. I'd really hate to think that key legal decisions are being made by people with no more of a legal background than my own."

"Why not?" Moore asked. "You couldn't do any worse. This friend of mine was still subbing in the courtroom during a sentencing on a guy he had investigated a few months before. It was a manslaughter pled down to negligent homicide. Anyway, this guy was drivin' down a residential street doin' at least 40 miles an hour, drunk as hell and no headlights on."

"Why in the hell would someone drive around with no headlights?" Keller thought aloud.

"That's a good question," Moore responded, pointing at Keller. "When the cop caught up to him, he asked the same thing." Moore tried unsuccessfully to repress a laugh. "I'm sorry. I know it's not funny. But on the other hand, it is. This idiot tells the cop he was driving with no lights on so the cops wouldn't notice him."

"Christ!" Crew blurted.

*Information and Belief*

"Anyway, this guy hits a car and kills the teenage girl who's driving. So, my buddy does the report. This guy has four prior drunk driving convictions and at least seven driving while license suspended tickets. And, of course, his license was suspended when it happened. And, just for good measure, he violated his probation three out of the four times."

"I'm almost afraid to hear," Natalie said tentatively.

"And your fear is justified," Moore answered. "Judge Ash sentenced him to probation and AA classes. So then, there's this loud scream from the back of the court. It's the victim's father. He starts yellin' about how this guy killed his daughter and what a joke this system is if it lets a killer like this guy go."

"Which is exactly what I'd be yelling," Crew said emphatically.

"No doubt," Moore agreed. "So he keeps yellin' about this guy's past record and that he's bound to go on killin' people if someone doesn't stop him. So Judge Ash has the victim's father jailed for two days for contempt of court. Which, by the way, is one day longer than his daughter's killer spent."

"Doesn't that figure," Natalie said with disgust. "The first person he has the guts to put in jail in years is a victim."

"I don't think it has anything to do with guts," Keller contradicted. "Incarceration requires more paperwork, thus more time, from the judge. And, yes, some of them are just that lazy."

"Every month for the past two years I've heard someone say that guy's announced his retirement," Crew said dejectedly. "But he just never leaves. The clerks say he's so burned out, he just goes through the motions. He doesn't even read the pre-sentence reports anymore."

"He's in good company there," Natalie commented. "Last week I got a probation order back from Judge Henman's courtroom with a condition that the defendant not have any contact with his wife except during child visitation."

"Yeah, but that's not too uncommon for the court to try to protect the victim with a no-contact order," Bradner conceded.

"Believe me," Natalie said, "if the wife had been the victim, I would have been the first one to request the order. But this was a bar fight. His wife didn't have anything to do with it. This guy is happily married, but technically in violation of his probation by living with his wife, until I can find a diplomatic way to get the order rescinded without making the judge look bad."

"Oh yes indeed," Moore agreed. "If the judge thinks you're pointing out his mistakes, you're life's hell from here on out." He raised an eyebrow. "On the other hand, I know a lot of guys who'd pay good money to be court-ordered out of the home."

"There's a new business for ya," Bradner laughed. "Custom amended orders. You could sell 'em and make a mint."

"Honest, honey," Moore said with a smile and a shrug, "the judge ordered that I live with my buddies and eat nothing but take-out."

"Mr. Crew, Ms Fisher, Ms Keller, Mr. Bradner...you have clients," the disembodied voice announced.

*Information and Belief*

# Chapter 18

The group split, with Bradner and Crew headed toward the coffee pot for a refill while Keller and Natalie walked to the lobby.

"Let's make it interesting," Keller said. "We'll start the morning with a friendly wager."

"I'm up for it," Natalie responded, always quick to divert her attention from the stress of a busy report day.

"By the sounds of the page there are at least four clients in the lobby."

"Sounds reasonable," Natalie concurred.

"How many are sex offenders?"

Natalie laughed.

"Well?"

"OK, OK," Natalie stalled. "Let's see, I didn't see Mr. King last week, so he's due. And when he's due, he's usually first. So I know there's at least one." She paused. "I'm going for the clean sweep," she said boldly. "All four."

"I'll go with three," Keller countered as she swung open the door.

Natalie followed her into the waiting room. She gave Keller a knowing smile. Mr. King sat at the far left. Keller's senior citizen rapist was three seats away.

"Don't get cocky yet," Keller said under her breath as they examined the sign-in sheet. "I'll check Crew's guy, you check Bradner's."

"I know Bradner's," Natalie responded. "Took his report two weeks ago when he was on annual leave."

"And?" Keller asked as she put a line through her client's name.

"I'm still in the ball game," she said softly as she crossed King's name off the list. "Mr. King," she called.

The stocky man with neatly combed blond hair popped out of his chair.

"Hi," Natalie greeted him. "How are you at this early hour?"

"Fine," he responded. "And you?"

"Mr. Baurn," Keller called with less enthusiasm.

The old man stood slowly and straightened the seam in this trousers. "Good morning."

69

"Morning," she muttered as she motioned for him to proceed down the hall.

Once seated in the bull pen, Keller stepped to Crew's desk and opened his roadbook to the appropriate page. "Damn," she said.

"Go ahead and finish filling that out," Natalie told Mr. King as she stood. "I'll be right back."

"I'm so sorry," King said remorsefully. "I'll take some blank forms home and have it filled out before I come next time. You're just so fast, I didn't have time."

"It's not a problem. Take your time."

She joined Keller. "Want to go double or nothin' that they all brought their check stubs and money orders?"

"Forget it," she said, slapping the cover of the roadbook closed. "Anal little bastards probably have every check stub they ever got from the age of 16 in reverse chronological order in their back pockets just in case we decide to ask about it."

"Every caseload needs at least 10 of these guys."

"Don't worry," Keller responded. "I don't anticipate a shortage any time soon."

The two returned to their desks.

"Any police contacts or changes?" Natalie asked King while seating herself.

"None whatsoever," he responded with a smile.

"Did you bring your paycheck stub?"

"Yes," he replied amicably. "I have everything you need right here." He placed several papers of varying sizes, with the largest on the bottom working to the top by size, fastened neatly at the upper left hand corner with a paper clip. "I brought my pay stub, a progress letter from the psychologist, and two money orders. One made out to the state for supervision fees and the other to the county for court costs."

"Wonderful," Natalie complimented him.

"And I wrote my docket number, file number, and your name as my supervising agent on the back. I noticed that you do that when you're processing them."

"Thank you. That's very considerate." She opened the thick black three-ring binder to the face sheet with King's general information. She glanced at the conditions. Psych treatment, costs,

## Information and Belief

fees, no contact with victim, victim's family, or any child unless supervised. She flipped past the cardboard face sheet to the attached running log of notes. The papers were color coded, the differing colors representing the assessed risk level. Mr. King was on pink paper. Maximum. All sex offenders start at maximum. She made the needed notations for this visit. Reports no police contacts or status changes, verified work and treatment.

"Is everything else OK?" she asked.

"Well, work is good. I like the treatment group you got me in. I think it's doing me a lot of good. I guess my only problem is that it's hard to get out twice a month to come here without anyone at work asking where I've been."

"I know its difficult," Natalie acknowledged. "But the supervision standards for someone on maximum status are two times a month in the office and two contacts a month by phone."

"Oh, I'm not complaining. I'm going to do whatever I need to do to get this whole thing behind me."

"Is there anything else?" Natalie asked as she closed the book.

"Well..." he started sheepishly.

"Go ahead," Natalie encouraged.

"It's my youngest daughter. She's been having a lot of trouble with her mother since our split up. She's been asking to come and spend weekends."

Natalie took a deep breath and shook her head. "Mr. King, this is old territory. You know you can't have any unsupervised contact with any minors."

"I understand that," he replied in a pleading tone. "But this isn't just any child. This is my daughter. They can't think I'd do anything to her."

Natalie sat quietly for a moment. *Keep an even, calm tone,* she thought. *Don't let your first client get you riled. That sets a hell of a tone for the day.* She cleared her throat. "Mr. King, your eldest daughter was the victim of this offense," she reminded.

"My step-daughter," he said defensively.

"Let's not split hairs, sir. You raised her from an infant. You're the only dad she ever knew."

"I'll do what I have to do," he responded softly. "But I just want you to know...I'm not like that. I wouldn't do that to one of my own kids. That's just...that's just sick."

Natalie stood to discourage any further discussion. "That's all we need today," she said conclusively. "You'll call me next Friday and I'll see you back here the Friday after."

Natalie escorted him to the lobby. She went to the window to check the sign-in sheet. A tall, muscular black man leaned on the counter, his arm covering the list, as he spoke loudly into the glass that separated himself from the receptionist.

"Do Mz. Kella know I'm here?" he barked.

"Yes, sir," the gentle voice, barely audible through the glass, replied. "I've already paged her.

"Well you need to be pagin' her again. I don't be havin' all day fo' dis shit."

"Excuse me," Natalie said calmly. "I just need to glance at that sheet under your arm for a second."

"This is bullshit," he protested. "How come she always be makin' me wait like dis?"

"She's with someone right now," Natalie explained. "But I'll let her know you're waiting when I go back Mr...Mr?"

"Johnson," he responded boldly. "Tommy Lee Johnson." He slid the clipboard down the counter.

She stopped the board just inches before it flew over the side. She was determined to foil his attempt at intimidation. She slowly walked toward him, meeting his glare with solid eye contact. She made a point of stepping several inches closer into his personal space than she sensed he was comfortable with. He shifted his weight, and his eyes left hers and scanned the room. She reached around him, taking a pencil from the counter, and returned to the clipboard that continued to lay on the far end. She ran her finger down the list, inwardly grateful that her hands were not shaking.

"Mr. Stalk," she called.

"Here," the young man responded, as though answering to a roll call, as he sprung to his feet and toward the door. He looked nervously at the large man as he sidestepped past him, like a high school student trying to escape the hall monitor when he's late to class.

"I'll let Ms. Keller know you're here, Mr. Johnson," Natalie said politely as she closed the door.

"It's good to see you could make it this morning, Mr. Stalk," she said in a sincere tone.

"What's that guy's problem?" he asked with annoyance. "I only got here 10 minutes ago and I signed in before him."

"Ms. Keller," Natalie announced in a rather formal fashion as she passed Donna's desk, "A rather surly Mr. Tommy Lee Johnson would like you to know that he doesn't have all day."

"Lovely," she said with disdain as she handed the man at her desk a card. "You need to call this number and get back in treatment…"

"Have a seat Mr. Stalk," Natalie said routinely as she opened the roadbook, scanned the face sheet to review the conditions, then turned to the notes. "Any police contacts or status changes?"

"No changes," he replied as he laid his report form on the desk along with his check stub.

Natalie looked at the report form to make sure his verbal response matched what was in writing. Some of the more seasoned probationers could spot a lazy agent and would write a different address or note police contact on the written form. When the agent noticed the change or found out about the arrest later, the probationer would then say, "I told you about that. See, its even on my report form."

"My car didn't cost as much as I thought," he said as he produced a money order from his wallet.

"I'm glad to hear that," Natalie responded, checking the year-to-date gross income on his check. "It looks like you've been getting a lot of overtime."

"Yeah, I can't complain about that. It sure is coming at a good time of year."

"OK," Natalie said as she examined the money order. "$100 toward restitution."

"Yeah," he said bitterly. "Her whole damn car wasn't worth $100. I can't believe the judge is soakin' me for $750 for that piece of shit Tercel."

"It's only money, Mr. Stalk. In any other county in the state, they'd never have pled you back down to misdemeanor stalking after that first conviction."

"That first conviction was a bunch of crap," he said bitterly. "It used to be no problem to call a girl who wanted to break up with ya to try to talk her out of it. Now, people make a federal case out of everything. You should have heard those Westland cops laugh when they booked me on stalking charges. You know...with my last name and all. Real mature. They're lucky I don't prosecute them for harassment."

"Granted, having a bunch of juvenile cops make fun of your name can be irritating," Natalie agreed. "But it really doesn't hold a candle to following a woman around and shooting up her car when she doesn't return your calls."

Stalk rolled his eyes. "You make it sound so dramatic. I put a couple of bullets into a piece of shit car."

She stood, returning the pay stub as they walked to the lobby. "See you back here the second Friday of next month."

Natalie ran her finger down the sign-in sheet. Things were getting backed up early. The lobby was packed. She could feel angry eyes cut her in half. Most belonging to people who didn't know her name. She felt a little more prepared for this than the other agents. She'd experienced the same angry stares at a gay pride march a few years back. Although the origin of the anger was different, it was still anger. She ran a line through the next name and called, "Mr. Abeeb."

A slightly built Arabic man in his early 40s stood, walked to the small table jutting from the wall, and set the outdated copy of the *Ladies Home Journal* on the edge. "Good morning," he said with a smile.

"Good morning," she returned as he followed her to her desk.

"You look very nice today," he complimented her.

"Thank you," she replied in a tone that recognized the statement but did not solicit another. She opened the roadbook. "Oh, yeah," she said softly as her gaze was greeted by the notation in red ink under the last drug test.

"Excuse me?" he apologized. "I didn't hear you."

"We have something to talk about, Mr. Abeeb." She took his report form. "But let's do this in order so I don't forget anything."

"I'm not understanding," he responded quizzically.

"Any police contacts or status changes?"

"No."

*Information and Belief*

She made the notation. "Do you have your rent form and monthly income statement so we can verify that you're still running the party store?"

"Oh, yes." He handed her an envelope from his inner jacket pocket.

She examined the papers, then wrote 'Employment verified via monthly income statement.' "Did you bring your money orders?"

He paused. "I didn't have time to stop and get one."

Natalie tapped her pen on the roadbook, not looking up. *God, this'll be one long day*, she thought. Keeping her tone even, she responded, "Mr. Abeeb. You own a party store. Isn't that where people typically go to get money orders? I mean, it's not like it's miles out of your way."

He looked at her blankly.

"No payment on costs or fees this day. Instructed to bring payment next report," she wrote. "Now, with that business aside, we need to talk about the results of your last drug test. They returned positive for cocaine."

He stared at her without responding.

"So, what's going on, Mr. Abeeb?"

"I'm not understanding. What does this mean?"

"It means we sent the sample you provided to the lab and it returned positive for cocaine, sir."

"What do you mean by sample?"

"Mr. Abeeb, please don't play the 'I don't understand' game. You've been in this country longer than I've been alive."

He said nothing.

"The last time you were here, I had you sign a paper and we gave you a bottle. I'm sure you remember. As I recall, you were not at all pleased that I had to send an agent with you into the bathroom to…"

"Oh yes. I know what you are talking about now."

"Good. Anyway, that test came back positive for cocaine."

"So, what does that mean?"

"It means that you've been using cocaine, sir. Since you were convicted of selling drugs out of your store, we consider drug use a serious matter. People who are using have a tendency to sell in order to…"

"This is ridiculous!" he said loudly, slapping his hand on the desk.

The room, clamorous with activity moments before, fell instantly silent. Crew came from behind his desk, leaving his client in mid-sentence. He walked to Natalie's filing cabinet, placed his arm across the top, leaned his tall, rugged frame slightly forward, and asked, "Ms. Fisher, would you happen to have a travel permit handy?"

Abeeb looked nervously at the imposing figure before him. Natalie pulled the form out of the left-hand desk drawer and handed it to Crew. With her back to Abeeb, she gave Crew a knowing smile. If he had said anything directly to Abeeb, it could have caused Abeeb to think she couldn't handle herself. Crew had just made his presence known.

"I apologize for the raising of my voice," Abeeb said quietly as Crew returned to his desk. "But you must understand, I am Moslem. We do not use drugs. It is forbidden."

"Mr. Abeeb, we have a good lab. The test came back positive for cocaine. If you don't use drugs..."

"I've been doing some reading," he interrupted. "There is a lawsuit going on right now between some bank tellers and their bank. They were fired because they tested positive for cocaine on their random drug test."

Natalie set her pen down, leaning back in her chair. "And?"

"The tellers are proving that they work in an area where lots of drug money comes in. They have to count this money. It gets on their hands and goes into their bodies through their pores."

Natalie closed her eyes and rubbed her temples. "You know, Mr. Abeeb, for a guy who don't know what I'm talking about, you sure are well read on the subject."

"What do you mean?"

Natalie sighed. "What I mean, sir, is that you're going to be drug tested again today. If you test positive, I'll request an amended order mandating that you enter treatment."

"Drug treatment! I am not one of those low life drug addicts. I'm a respected businessman."

"With all due respect, sir, you're here for selling drugs. Most people don't consider that a respected business."

"Selling the drugs and taking drugs are not the same thing. If I didn't sell them, you would. Someone's going to."

*Information and Belief*

"First of all, sir, I wouldn't be selling them. Seeing the world that way is mighty convenient when you want to make money." Natalie stopped herself. *Damn. Baited again.* She eased her tone. "But this isn't a moral debate. The point is, you tested positive for drugs. If you test positive for drugs again, you'll likely be ordered into treatment."

"But what am I to do?" he protested. "Sell my business? I have to take in the money. If the money has drugs on it..."

"Mr. Abeeb," Natalie interrupted. "A person can smoke crack cocaine all day, every day for two weeks, 24 hours, non-stop, and will only test positive for 48 hours after the last time he smoked it. The traces that would enter your blood wouldn't hang on from the time you left your store to the time you got here." She finished filling in the blanks on the chain of custody form and turned it for his signature.

"I will be vindicated when the tellers win their suit," he mumbled as he scribbled his signature.

Natalie escorted him back to the lobby. "OK, you know the procedure. Wait in the lobby 'til the tech calls your name." She placed his form on the specimen desk located near the exit to the lobby. "Looks like there's two ahead of you. It shouldn't be long."

Mr. Abeeb and Natalie separated in the lobby. He lifted a copy of *Better Homes and Gardens* from the table as Natalie went to the sign-in sheet.

"Why are these types of magazines the only things out here?" he complained.

"What do you mean?" Natalie asked. Although she already knew what he was referring to, she couldn't resist turning the question game back on him.

"These kind?" he said, holding the magazine up. "*Ladies Home Journal. Better Homes and Gardens. Red Book. Glamour.*"

"What about them?" Natalie crossed the next name off the list.

"Yeah, well what do ya want Abdul, *Soldier of Fortune*?!" a raspy voice shot back from the other side of the room.

Natalie knew the voice before she turned to face her next client. Marc Snyder. She remembered how the abrasive tone had sent a chill down her spine the day of her pre-sentence interview with him.

Snyder continued. "So, this welfare wench thinks she can let her little picaninny run around like some tribal thing. So, I say, 'Hey bitch, if you don't whip your little nigger and teach her some goddamn respect, I will. Next thing you know, some nigger cop is puttin' me in cuffs sayin' there's some law called Felony Ethnic Intimidation. Like this isn't America anymore and I can't say what I feel. It's a goddamn police state. That's what it is."

A few snickered. Several others stiffened in their chairs, anticipating conflict.

"What is it you are meaning by this?!" Abeeb shouted as he took several quick steps toward Snyder.

Snyder threw his head back and displayed a cocky smile. "I didn't mean anything, Abdul. Just tryin' to determine your literary preference."

"That's enough," Natalie said in a quiet but stern voice.

"I will not be spoken to in this manner," Abeeb stated proudly.

"What are you gonna do about it?" Snyder challenged.

"Neither of you are going to do anything about it unless you want a free ride to the Lincoln Park PD," Natalie barked. "Mr. Abeeb, please have a seat. Mr. Snyder, step into the office. You're next."

"But you can not allow…"

"Mr. Abeeb," Natalie said, regaining control of her tone. "Please let me handle this in a more suitable place than the lobby."

"But…"

"Mr. Abeeb," she interrupted. Have I ever lied to you?"

"What?" he asked.

"Have I ever lied to you," she repeated.

"No."

"Then please trust that I'll take care of it." She turned to Snyder. "This way Mr. Snyder," she directed, motioning toward the door.

They entered and walked silently to her desk.

"Those desert types are real excitable," he said with an antagonistic smile.

"Your behavior came very close to endangering the safety of everyone in this office, sir." Natalie pulled her bottom desk drawer open, fingering several files before finding the one labeled Max Sup. Level. She removed the pink sheet, placed it on the desk and leaned back in her chair. "So, what exactly were you trying to do out there?"

"Who, me? he said in a mocking tone, throwing his hands up.

"I've got all day, sir."

## Information and Belief

The two sat in silence for a little over 30 seconds. Then Snyder let out a laugh that was slightly too loud and too long for Natalie's liking. "Oh, come on little lady. What's the big deal? I was just playin' with ol' Abdul for a bit."

"I'm not altogether sure that he appreciates being called Abdul when you consider that's not his name. As for the crack about the *Soldier of Fortune* magazine..."

"I know where this is leadin'," he said sternly. He leaned toward her. His tone took on a quiet, conspiratorial tone. "If you even think of violatin' my probation, my lawyer'll be all over ya. Ya can't send a guy to jail for gettin' a fella's name wrong. It's not like I threatened him."

"You're right." Natalie wheeled herself three feet to the left, opened the bottom file drawer, and removed the folder marked Snyder, Marc. She picked up her pen and opened the roadbook. "Let's start from the beginning. Any police contacts or status changes?"

Snyder, displaying a victorious smile, replied. "None."

She made the notations. "Employment verification and money orders?"

He pulled two money orders from his wallet. "The problem with those types is that they get everything too easy. They come to this country with their family's money, buy a store, and think they own the damn world." He signed the orders. "Well, every once in a while, someone's gotta let 'em know that Dearborn ain't the world."

"Employment verification?" Natalie repeated.

"I think I washed that with my other pair of jeans," he said with a laugh. "Since the old lady left, things ain't been runnin' too smooth."

Natalie pulled his file from under the roadbook, opened it to his probation order, and placed it before him.

"What's this?" he asked warily.

"I figured you were probably going to want to see that before we're through."

"What're ya talkin' about?"

"I'll start by letting you know that you're right. I'd get thrown out of court on my ear if I tried to violate your probation based on what happened in the lobby. I mean, we both know you were trying to goad that guy into a fight, but your lawyer could clean that up."

"It's a free country last time I looked. I'll say what I want."

"However, based on your behavior, I can increase your risk classification from Medium to Maximum. Which is why I have this pink paper."

"Oh, no," he said, feigning fear. "Not pink paper." He laughed. "I guess I can live with fag-colored paper in my file."

"I'm glad to see you're taking this so well." She noted the change in classification on the roadbook face sheet. "I'll see you next week."

He stood quickly, checking his wallet before returning it to his rear pocket. "You mean next month."

"No, sir, I mean next week. Unemployed people under maximum supervision need to report every week."

"What?! This ain't right. You can't make me come down here every week."

Natalie pointed to the probation order which lay on the desk before him. "Read standard condition #3."

"It says you can make me report monthly," he said brashly.

"Read the whole sentence," she said calmly.

He read aloud. "You will report monthly…" He lowered his voice. "Or as often as directed, either in person or in writing, as directed by the probation department."

"And, as often as directed, in your case, means once a week while unemployed."

"But I have a job," he protested. "You know I have a job."

"I don't know anything that's not verified, sir. When you bring in verification, I'll reduce your in-person reports to every other week. Of course, you'll have to call and check in on the off weeks."

"This is harassment," he hissed. "You can't do this."

"Sir, there are very few things I can do. But I assure you, this is one of them." She stood and closed the file.

"Well, I'll send someone by this afternoon with a copy of my check stub."

"I'm sorry, sir. I can't let you do that."

"Why not?" His arrogant tone had diminished to a whine.

"I've got 30 people scheduled today. If I let everyone come back who couldn't remember to bring their stuff, I'd have 60." She returned the file to the drawer. "I'll see you next week."

*Information and Belief*

# Chapter 19

    Natalie leaned back in her chair, running her hands along the coarse fabric of the arms. She closed her eyes and took a deep breath, taking full advantage of the 10 a.m. lull. The chair had been a gift from an agent who fled Wayne County for a rural post in the northern part of the state. The gift was based more on practicality than any strong bond between the two. They were both a little under 5-feet 4-inches. The chair sat too close to the ground for most.
    She closed her eyes and took a deep breath, then slowly released it. Every report day she tried to take time to unwind in this manner. As she relaxed, her mind wandered back to the agent she had dubbed "Bam Bam." He was undersized, with hair so blond it almost appeared white in the summer months, and she likened his temper tantrums to those of the cartoon character on *The Fintstones*, who rocked the house with his club when he didn't get his way. When the department of corrections altered policy to limit the number of handguns carried by a field agent to one, she referred to it as the "Bam Bam" ruling. A former small-town police officer, he felt vulnerable when armed with only one gun and mace while working in the big city of Detroit. It was common knowledge that he never adhered to the new policy. It was also common knowledge that he would "accidentally" allow his jacket to fall open, revealing his weapon, whenever he was in a tough neighborhood.
    "Fisher. You all right?"
    Natalie opened her eyes to see Joan Ballard. She was fully attired in a bulky winter coat, scarf and mittens. Natalie could feel the fresh cold emanate from her body.
    "Just taking a quick mental break. What brings you to rookie row? Slummin'?"
    Ballard looked tentatively around the room. "Come with me to my office for a minute. I've got something to show you."
    "Sure." She picked up her coffee cup and followed the senior agent down the hall. "Did you pick out the new wall paper for your kitchen?"

They entered Ballard's office. "It's nothing like that," Ballard said softly, motioning her closer. "We've got to keep it down. These offices aren't much better for privacy than the bull pen."

Natalie leaned in. "What's up?"

"I just got back from taking Elds to her disciplinary hearing. She told me on the way that she'd let you in on it."

"Yeah," Natalie acknowledged with a smile. "So, did she get enough time off to go to Florida?"

"She got enough time off to live in Florida. They fired her!"

"What?!"

"Can you believe it?" Ballard tossed her keys on her desk. "She's worked here for what?...eight, almost nine years, and they fired her in less than three minutes. I didn't even have time to finish the chapter I started in my book."

"What kind of a hearing is that?"

"She said they told her, 'This isn't a hearing. Our investigation has been completed.' They rattled off chapter and verse of the work rules like they were quoting scripture, and that was it. Escorted to the door. Have a nice life."

"Where is she now?"

"Cleaning out her desk," Ballard replied glumly. "She just wanted me to tell you before you heard it through the grapevine."

"Maybe I can still catch her before she goes," Natalie said, stepping toward the door.

"No. She doesn't want to see anyone right now. She's real shook up. But she said she might stop at the bar tonight, so try to clear a few hours this evening if you can. I'm sure she'll need people around if she shows up."

"And if she doesn't?"

"I'll head to her house and make sure she's OK."

Natalie sighed. "This is a tough call. I want to show her I'm with her, but I suppose we should give her some space if she needs it."

"I know what you mean. But all we can really do is go by the cues she's giving. I've known her for a good many years. She'll let us know what she needs."

"Ms. Keller, Ms. Fisher, and Mr. Crew...You have clients," the gentle voice from above urged.

# Chapter 20

"...so anyway, I'm just waitin' on my disability to kick in."

"I'm sorry, what?" Natalie was embarrassed, realizing she had let her mind wander. She glanced at her watch. It was 3:50. She knew she'd better get with it and pick up the pace. The lobby would pack up between 4:15 and 5 with people who were working and people who wanted to get lost in the shuffle of people who were working. The latter being the druggies who hoped she'd be lazy and wouldn't drop them at 4:50 and risk leaving after 5.

"I said," the young, narrow-faced black man repeated in an agitated tone, "I'm not workin' 'cause I'm waitin' on my disability."

"Oh, I'm sorry. I forgot. What was your disability?"

"I gets angry all the time. I can't keeps a job 'cause I gets angry all the time."

"You can get disability for that?" Natalie asked. *Guess we won't be seeing Agent Moore around when news of this breaks*, she thought with a smile.

"My friend's cousin been gettin' on for it."

"Hum," Natalie said, making the notation. "You know, sometimes when you hear these friend of a friend stories, there's more going on than you know about."

"What you mean?" he barked.

Natalie looked at her watch. "I guess I mean that if anyone asks me, I'll be able to tell them that you do get angry easily," she said with a laugh. "Let's move on."

He laughed. "I don't mean to be gittin' up in your face or nothin'. But I be wantin' what's mine."

"Fair enough." She ran her finger down the page until it rested on the red ink. "You tested positive for marijuana again."

"This just ain't right," he protested. "I told you I don't be smokin' no weed."

"Mr. Thompson, we've gone down this road before. You say you don't smoke weed, but you keep coming back dirty. I know you don't think weed is a big deal. But you're on felony probation and you can't afford this kind of..."

"Now just hold on." He held his hand up like a traffic cop. "I know what you're gonna be sayin. But I gots it figured. I don't be smokin' dis shit, but I know why I been testin' dirty."

Natalie looked at her watch again. 4:15. "OK. Why are you coming back dirty?"

"You see, my girl, she be smoking dope like she gonna die tomorra' or somethin'."

"Second hand smoke doesn't show up on the screen, Mr. Thompson."

"Naw, naw," he said, shaking his head vigorously. "It ain't nothin' like dat. You see, we be gettin' it on maybe two or three times a day."

Natalie paused. "What?"

"You know what I be talkin' 'bout. Don't be playin' like you don't."

Natalie leaned forward. "Are you trying to say that having sex with someone who smokes marijuana is causing you to test positive?"

"It's not just sex," he said quietly. "You see, my baby just ain't happy lest...well...you know."

"I know...what?"

"What I'm sayin' is...it be the kinda sex where..." He looked around the room. "I don't know why you be makin' me say it. I'm talkin' 'bout oral sex."

"Woooow, hold it," Natalie said abruptly. "Too much information." She buried her face in her hands for a moment, then rubbed her temples. "Mr. Johnson, this is, by far, the most ridiculous thing I've heard since..."

"What you mean," he said defensively. "If I can catch the herpes that way, then why can't I get dat like dat?"

"Herpes is a sexually transmitted disease, sir." She could hear Bradner and Crew attempting to suppress their laughter. Failing miserably.

"Aw, man," he protested, throwing his head back and wincing. "You just be havin' it in fo' me."

"Ms. Fisher, Ms. Keller, Mr. Crew, Mr. Wood and Mr. Bradner, you have clients," the soft voice announced.

"Mr. Jonhson, I'm under no obligation to prove to you that I don't, as you put it, have it in for you." She paused. "However, I've got to give you credit. That was the most innovative excuse I've heard in months. I mean, the poppie seed roll gets old after awhile. So, this is what I'm going to do. I won't drop you today. You come back in 30 days and drop at your next report. You abstain from...whatever activity you honestly believe makes you test positive from drugs."

They stood and walked down the hall.

"OK," he said as he opened the door to the lobby. "But you gonna be havin' to 'splain to my girl..."

"No, no, no!" Natalie said adamantly as she walked to the sign-in sheet. "I don't have to do anything. I'm not on probation. You are."

She crossed the next name off the list. "Mr. Gonzalez," she announced.

She lead the young, Hispanic man to her desk. "How are you, Mr. Gonzalez?"

"I'm fine, and you?"

"I'm OK." She opened the roadbook to his page. "Be a lot better in about a half hour," she added with a laugh.

"I don't blame you there," he responded with a smile. "I always forget who to make these out to," he added, producing two money orders from his back pocket.

"Damn!" Natalie said, snatching a yellow post-it note from the left side of her file tray.

"I'm sorry!" he replied with astonishment.

"Oh, I didn't mean you," Natalie said apologetically. "It's this. I forgot to call and set up this appointment." She handed him a pen. "Make the larger one out to Wayne County Adult Probation, or W.C.A.P. for short, and the second one to the State of Michigan."

He took the pen. "Got it."

"I'll just make this call while you do that." She swiveled her chair around, rolled the two feet needed to reach the shelf she had created by placing a plank on top of two half-sized filing cabinets, and grabbed the file labeled *James, Eric* out of the rack. She leafed through several pages, found the number on the conviction and referral slip, and dialed it.

"Don't forget to put your file number and docket somewhere on the front," she reminded Gonzalez as the phone rang at the other end.

"Hello."

"Hello, is..." Natalie paused as she looked at the family information section of the workbook. "Is Ms. Newkirk in please?"

"This is Mrs. Newkirk."

"Hi, this is Ms. Fisher with the Probation Department. I was given this number by your grandson, and..."

"Oh yes, Eric said you'd be calling," the voice said in a pleasant tone.

"Yes ma'am. I was wondering if I could set up a time to see you on Monday? I just need to stop in to see where he's living, and confirm some family information with you. It shouldn't take more than 15 minutes."

"That would be fine. I'll be home all day. What time can I expect you?"

Natalie ran her finger down her calendar. Possibly a 9 a.m. pre-sentence. Then she'd have to run down today's no-shows. "How would sometime between 2 and 3 in the afternoon be?"

"That'll be fine. I'll expect you then."

"Thank you. I look forward to meeting you then. Goodbye."

"Do I write those numbers on the front or back?" Gonzalez asked.

"Huh?"

"The file number and docket. I know you always tell me to write it on the front, but I saw a sign in the lobby on the drop box that says to write it on the back."

"I know," she conceded. "But I've learned from trying to run down lost orders in the past that they tell you to write on the back, but they only make a copy of the front. The person who wrote the policy never talked to the people in bookkeeping. Trust me."

"OK."

"Now," Natalie said, picking up her pen and moving the James file off her roadbook. "Any police contacts or status changes."

"None," he replied proudly.

Natalie began to make the notation, then realized she had spelled contacts, "contcats". From her drawer she took a bottle of green-out, as Gonzalez was on minimum supervision and therefore on green paper. It was late in the day and, as usual, her words were beginning to betray her. *OK*, she thought as she methodically painted over the error.

She knew from painful experience that trying to force the words just made it worse. Through the years, she had learned a few tricks in the never-ending battle of this love/hate relationship she had with the English language. The act of whiting out was more a stalling technique than a cosmetic repair. It slowed her brain down and prevented "the panic." The panic was her term for a state of mind experienced before she had learned to hold her own in the battle. In her youth, as a green soldier in the battle, she tried to plow through, writing faster or sloppier. The letters seemed to develop a life of their own, dancing around the page, forming combinations over which she had no control.

"Bullshit!" a youthful voice protested from Crew's side of the divider. "I told you when I called that I had surgery on my leg and had to stay off it for a week. Where do you get off telling me to come in and see you or go to jail?"

"Mr. Mills, I never told you that you'd go to jail. I don't have the power to send anybody to jail. Only the court..."

"Look at this!" the voice said. Natalie could hear paper rattling.

She slid her chair out and to the right to see around the orange cube wall. A young, bearded man sat in the chair placed in front of Crew's desk. He held a set of crutches by the handbars up vertically next to him on the right side, while his right leg, sporting a removable fabric brace with Velcro strips, stuck straight out and to the left. He put his weight on his good leg and pulled himself up by the handle of the crutches just far enough to slap a piece of paper on the desk. He winced as he eased himself back in the chair. "The one on top is the note from my doctor saying I need complete bed rest for two weeks. I told you that when I called you..."

"Mr. Mills," Crew interrupted. "You called me from a pay phone to tell me you can't leave your house."

"So?"

"So, do you keep a pay phone in your house? If you can't leave your house, why did you call from a pay phone?"

"Because my phone's out of order."

Crew picked up the phone, glanced at the face sheet in his roadbook, and dialed.

"What are you..."

"Hello. Ms. Mills. It's Mr. Crew. Jerry's here with me now and I was just calling because he had a concern that there was something wrong with your phone so…Oh, no problems. I see." He listened for a moment. "Yes ma'am. I was just calling to make sure everything's OK. You have a good day. Bye."

He hung up and leaned forward. "The phone seems fine. Your mom doesn't seem to know what you're talking about."

"Look!" the man yelled. "I've just been to the doctor. He knows the stress I'm under and I'm on medication. He said it could make me act funny. I can't be held responsible for my actions."

"What kind of medicine?"

"Xanax. He put me on Xanax 'cause I've been depressed."

Crew picked up his pen. "What medication are you on? Zantac? Isn't that a stomach medication?"

"No. Xanax. It's a nerve medication. My nerves are real bad right now."

"How do you spell that?"

"What do you mean, how do you spell that? Don't you people have to go to school for this job?"

"Mr. Mills, you sound like a man desperate to change the subject. What it boils down to is this. You have to report to probation one time a month. Each month, you come up with a new reason for why you can't do that." Crew turned back the pages of his notes. "Last month, 'Subject did not report. Home call conducted. States he lost appointment card.' The month before, 'Subject did not report. Home call conducted. States he started a new job. Unable to provide writer with name and address of employer as he states he works off the books.' The month before, 'Subject did not report. Home call conducted.'" He looked up. "Do I really need to go on?"

"The reason that I had to go to the pay phone is that the phone at my girlfriend's is out of order. That's where I've been staying. You spend so much time at my mother's house, I've had to go on medication and move."

"I only go to your mother's house when you don't show up here."

"This is bullshit. You've just got it in for me. "I've been on probation before and no other P. O. has come to my house."

"I can't speak to what other agents do, sir. I'm just doing my job. I have to know where you live. And that means where you lay your

*Information and Belief*

head at night. That's a condition of probation clearly listed on your probation order. So, if you're staying with your girlfriend now, I need the address and we need to set a time for a home call."

"I don't know the address right off the top of my head. I'll call you with it."

"There's no need for that," Crew said as he stood up. "That was her in the lobby, right? Let's just go get it from her on your way out."

"You can't go ask her."

"Why?"

"Because it's another girlfriend I've been staying with and she'll get pissed off."

Crew sat back down and silently looked at the ceiling for a moment. "So what you're saying," he summarized, returning his focus to the young man in the chair, "is, while at girlfriend #1's house, you realized that you had to call me, so you got girlfriend #2 to come and get you, take you to a pay phone and call me, despite the considerable pain you were in. Then, when I told you that you had to come here today or your probation would be violated, you had girlfriend #2 take you from the pay phone to this office."

Mills sat in silence for a moment, processing what he just heard. "Yeah, that's exactly what happened."

"And," Crew continued, "You don't want me to go ask girlfriend #2 the address of where you're living, because she doesn't know about girlfriend #1. Right?"

Mills smiled. "Right."

"Does girlfriend #1 know about girlfriend #2?"

Mills thought, then answered. "No. Mr. Crew," he continued with a sly smile. "There's no law against having two girlfriends."

"I guess the one thing that I don't understand is this, Sir. If girlfriend #2 doesn't know about girlfriend #1, and girlfriend #1 doesn't have a phone...how did you contact #2 and get her to pick you up at #1's house. After all, you're unable to walk any distance."

Mills thought. "I called her from a neighbor's phone."

"Then why didn't you just call me from that neighbor's phone instead of calling #2 to have her drive you to a pay phone and..."

"Knock it off!" Mills yelled, jumping to his feet. He and Crew seemed to realize that he was standing firmly on both legs at the same time. He jerked his weight off the bandaged leg. "You've got me so

89

mad, I went and stood on my bad leg. I'll probably have to go back to the doctor now."

"That's a good idea," Crew said, handing him back his papers. "After all, this two-week medical excuse is dated a month and a half ago. It's high time you had that thing re-checked."

"I'm sick of this shit," Mills snarled, pointing his finger just inches from Crew's face. "You stay away from my house, stay away from my mother, stay away from my girlfriend. If I see you outside of this building, there's gonna be trouble."

Natalie jumped to her feet. She found herself two steps behind Wood as they approached the confrontation.

"Are you threatening me?" Crew maintained his position, looking past the finger and into the man's eyes.

"I'm just telling you to keep your ass in this office or there'll be trouble. I'm on medication. No one's gonna hold me responsible for what I do."

"Sounds like a threat to me," Wood said.

The young man snapped around, almost tripping on his crutches. He looked nervously from the face of Wood, to Natalie, and then back to Crew.

"The problem is, Mr. Mills, you've claimed two different residences in the past five minutes. By policy, I now have to verify one."

The young man scratched his beard, looking puzzled. "What's that mean?"

"It means I now have to make another home call. I need a good address."

Mills bit his lip and looked at the wall. "Fine. Come to my mother's. That's where I live."

"I'll be out Monday," Crew said as he took a pen from his desk. "We'll just drop a quick urine and you'll be on your way."

"Why do I have to drop?" he protested. "I haven't had to drop in five months."

"Because you seem to be acting irrationally."

"I just told ya I'm on medication. Aren't you listening?"

"If that's the case, this will just help confirm it for us." He took a chain of custody form from the top of the cabinet. "You know the way," he prompted, pointing toward the hall.

Natalie and Wood exchanged expressions of relief as they parted company, returning to their desks.

"Sorry about the interruption, Mr. Gonzalez," she apologized. She quickly reviewed her notes. She spotted two errors she would have to correct later. "It looks like we've covered everything. If you keep paying at this pace and everything goes well, we could be looking at an early discharge for you."

"That would be great. I just want this over with."

"I can certainly understand that," Natalie agreed as the two stood and walked down the hall.

"This is just such a nightmare for me," he said, shaking his head as they neared the door to the lobby. "I'm the first member of my family to go to college. My family saved everything for that. Then I go and decide I'm just not gonna fit in at school without the right brand of pants and shirt. The next thing you know, I go from being the pride of my family to a felon."

"Well sir, if its a mistake you never make again, you'll bounce back. After all, you got HYTA. So if you don't have any more problems it'll come off your record."

"Yeah, but I heard that people can still find out about the arrest."

Natalie nodded her head in agreement. "Yes. Depending on their level of access, they can. Otherwise, someone could get their record cleared over and over just by saying that they'd never been arrested before."

"I can understand that. But its always been my dream to go into politics. But I could just see that headline now. 'Congressional candidate narrowly escapes felony conviction.'" He shrugged his shoulders, looking down in shame. "One stupid mistake and its all over."

"Yeah, sure," Natalie said slyly as she opened the door for him. "And Bill Clinton didn't inhale."

"Oh yeah," he said with a smile. "I guess if he can pull that off, there's still hope for me."

## Chapter 21

Natalie returned to the bull pen. Bradner was at his desk with Crew in "The Felon Chair." Wood and Fisher stood with their backs to the rear divider.

"Did you hear about Elds?" Keller asked as she joined them.

"Yeah. A couple of hours ago." Her heart sank as she replied. The hectic pace of the day had provided a comforting amnesia. "I can't believe they'd let her go over something so petty."

"What happened? I just heard it had something to do with a, quote, 'Improper relationship between herself and a probationer,' end quote.

"Who are we quoting?" Wood asked.

"I heard it from Supervisor Calab," Keller responded.

"That's a bunch of shit," Natalie said angrily. "What it boils down to is that she handed out a few business cards for a probationer who started his own repair shop."

"You can't be serious," Bradner stated with dismay.

"I don't know," Wood said hesitantly. "Even the appearance of impropriety needs to be avoided. She's been around long enough to know that anything we do can get twisted around if you give a con a chance to do it."

"But the cons aren't the ones doing the twisting," Natalie countered defensively. "I mean, we've all heard horror stories of what some agents have done, gotten caught at, and yet not fired."

"You're right," Keller agreed. "Like that supervisor who used her badge to get an after-hours visit with her jailbird boyfriend. She tried to tell the county deputies that she had to interview him for a violation hearing."

"I heard about that," Wood concurred. "Didn't they just transfer her to a different region?"

"And what about the legendary 'Ghost of Fort District,' Ms. Carter," Natalie added, pointing at the empty desk in the corner. "She drops in just long enough to let her pres hit the due date, then dumps 'em on someone else."

"All it takes is a doctor's note to go on medical," Wood noted. "At least she covers herself."

*Information and Belief*

"But that's just it," Natalie argued. "It's a guilty person who thinks about covering himself. Kay's got as good a reputation as anyone here. Wouldn't you like to think that your own boss and coworkers would give you the benefit of any doubt?" She backed toward her phone as she continued. "I mean, don't you think she's earned that?"

She dialed Gwen's number as the others dispersed.

"Gwen Taylor." The gentle voice betrayed a hint of weariness.

"Hi, its me."

"Hi. Where are you?"

"I'm still at the office."

"At 5:25?" Gwen asked with dismay. "Isn't there some bureaucratic rule against that?"

"Yeah. I'm expecting the civil service Gestapo to come storm trooping in at any minute. 'Put down ze penzils and step away from ze dezk.'" Natalie pointed her index finger with the thump up at Keller who laughed as she exited the bull pen with a quiet wave.

"That's a lousy German accent," Gwen said with a half-hearted chuckle.

"You missed the all-important visual," Natalie replied, her pout apparent in her tone. The discomforting silence on the other end of the line alerted her that Gwen was not in the mood to banter. She broke the silence. "OK. Anyway, the reason I called is to let you know I won't be coming directly home. It's a long story, but to sum it up, Elds got fired today."

"Fired! What happened?"

"I'll explain when I get home. But a few of us are going to meet at the bar. I mean, if that's not a problem for you. I know it's Friday night and all…"

"That's OK. I don't anticipate leaving here for at least another couple of hours," she said begrudgingly.

"Ouch!! I guess you're not having the greatest of days either."

"That would be an understatement."

"Hummm. God, I'm such a dope."

"What?"

"If I would have kept my mouth shut a few minutes and listened to your problems first, I could have acted all hurt and dejected because…you…instead of me…would have been the one to say she was working late on a Friday."

Gwen laughed. "Timing's everything."

"Damn! I could have gotten a dinner out of that at least."

"You could have come off as the considerate one and cashed in on the guilt. But," she breathed a dramatic sigh, "The moment is lost. But seriously, if you're going to the bar, don't forget that you've got a 30-minute drive home. Only one drink."

"No problem. See you in a few hours."

# Chapter 22

The sting of smoke assaulted Natalie's lungs as she entered the dimly lit sports bar. The lack of adequate lighting was contrasted by the excessive noise from pool tables, pinball machines, and the line of basketball hoops with musical backboards that blasted the University of Michigan fight song after every round. *God, I'm turning into such a wuss in my old age,* she thought as she rubbed her burning, watering eyes. Ten years prior she had been at the gay bar at least once a week, and smoking two packs a day. She'd always thought there was some strange correlation between lesbians and smoking. Although they were stereotyped as jocks, she had observed that the vast majority of lesbians she knew smoked. And although she'd never taken a census, she always felt the smoke level in any dyke bar bore out her theory.

But Gwen, nicoret gum in one hand and freshly squeezed vegetable juice in the other, had changed all of that. Smoking was the first major hurdle in their new relationship. By that time, Natalie had been up to almost two packs a day. Between the smell that lingered on every possession and the obvious physical toll that it was taking on Natalie's health, the habit had driven Gwen to distraction by the time she had laid down the ultimatum. Far from a health nut in her own right, Gwen indulged in the occasional cigarette with friends over a cocktail and could always find room for a sliver of pie. But, unlike Natalie, she had a take it or leave it relationship with her vices. Natalie knew that one cigarette would be the downfall of her new smoke-free life, and she would watch jealously as Gwen casually snitched one from a friend's pack. But, when pressured, Natalie would begrudgingly admit that she had felt a resurgence of energy after quitting. This, coupled with an increase in lung capacity, was the impetus for a morning workout routine that had caused her to become perhaps the first person to ever lose weight as a result of quitting smoking.

"Fisher! Over here!"

Natalie's eyes had adjusted enough to the darkness and smoke to allow her to detect a semi-standing, waving figure in the far corner.

Although visually unidentifiable, she knew the voice to be that of Joan Ballard.

Natalie descended the steps from the upper level, relieved to find that most of the smoke had not followed. Another benefit of being 5-feet 4-inches. She maneuvered through the sea of people, chairs, and tables, pretending not to notice some of the familiar faces of past and current probationers. One of the many downfalls of socializing so close to work.

"What took you so long?" Ballard chastised as she waved to the waitress.

"Report day. You remember Friday report days, right?"

"Never had them," Elds joined in. "When I started, nobody had Friday reports." She tipped her glass, finishing the last quarter-inch of beer. Natalie noted that two empty shot glasses also sat before her.

An uncomfortable silence followed. Natalie looked from Elds, to Ballard, then back to Elds. She could no longer endure it. "So, what's new?"

The three burst into laughter.

"Smooth, Fisher. Very smooth," Ballard said sarcastically.

"What can I say? Momma wasted a lot of money on social work school, I guess." Natalie again signaled the harried waitress. "I did great at empathetic listening. But, eventually, the time rolls around to where I've gotta talk. That's when I always get myself into trouble."

"What can I get you ladies?" The out-of-breath waitress, shouting to be heard as the crowd screamed their disapproval at a Red Wings missed scoring opportunity, leaned over Natalie's back.

"I'll have a Bud Light and another round for my friends," Natalie ordered.

"Busy night, ladies. Remind me." She removed the empties, balancing them precariously on her tray along with the discards from several other tables, while Elds ordered a Labats and a shot of peppermint schnapps. Natalie shuddered at the thought of that combination. Ballard ordered a Budweiser as Elds excused herself to the ladies' room.

Natalie and Ballard sat quietly until they were certain she was out of earshot. Natalie was the first to break the silence. "Where is everybody?"

*Information and Belief*

"I don't know. I'm pretty sure I got around to everyone before I cut out early for the day."

"I guess it was just too much of a last minute deal for most of them."

The waitress set the drinks on the table and Natalie quickly paid for them.

Ballard seemed equally annoyed by both the waitress's curt attitude and Natalie's response. "Christ, some of these people have worked with her for seven or eight years. If they can't put their petty little plans to hurry home for...I don't know...Dr. Quinn Medicine Woman. That really stinks."

"I think Dr. Quinn is Saturday night."

"That's not the point," Ballard said defensively.

"I know." Natalie leaned toward her friend. "I'm just trying to lighten things up a little."

Ballard reluctantly smiled. "OK. So I'm a little worked up." She looked toward the restrooms. When she saw no sign of her friend, she continued. "But I can't even imagine what this must be like for her. I mean, if I lost my job, things would be difficult, but I can always count on my husband. We could lose our standard of living maybe, but we wouldn't starve. She's on her own. You're not married. You should be able to relate to that."

Natalie felt suddenly angry. Not with Ballard, necessarily. But angry that, once again, her relationship with Gwen was discounted. This seemed like the classic, "do you or don't you," remind straight people that lesbians can't get married. It seemed to happen daily in one little way or another. Given the situation, "don't you", as usual, won out.

Elds returned, and the three woman worked on their drinks as she vented. "I just don't see what I did that was so wrong. Ten years ago, the department had the First Friend Policy."

"First Friend?" Natalie repeated.

"It was during the days when rehabilitation was the buzz word. As the parole slash probation agent, we were the convict's First Friend and role model as he attempted to live a crime-free life." She laughed and finished her shot, grimacing slightly as the hot liquid ran down her throat. "You know, rehabilitation is a great idea. But, like everything, the department took it to an extreme. That's why the convicts ate us alive back then. So now we live with the administration's knee-jerk reaction to that failure."

"Have you talked to the union?" Ballard asked.

"I have an appointment on Monday."

Natalie raised her glass, indicating a toast. "Here's to a very short paid vacation."

"That's right," Ballard added brightly. "Here's to reinstatement with back pay."

# Chapter 23

"Are you sure it's not too warm?" Natalie asked, placing her hand under the bathtub faucet.

Gwen placed her hand in the standing water at the other end. "It feels a little warm. We can let it cool for a few minutes while we get stuff together. Rowdy hates when the water's too cold."

"Rowdy hates baths altogether." Natalie dried her hands. "That should be about enough water. Any deeper and she's likely to panic."

"I'll get the kitty shampoo."

Natalie opened the cabinet under the sink. "Where are the old raggedy towels?"

"We don't keep them there anymore," Gwen yelled, digging through the hall closet.

Natalie felt a flash of irritation. This was one of the pet peeves she had about sharing a home. "We don't keep them there," she mumbled. "What's this 'we' stuff?" She stepped into the hall.

"They're in the cupboard in the utility room over the washer," Gwen yelled.

Natalie stood on her toes and reached in the cupboard overhead, her hand tapping two cold cans before locating a soft piece of terrycloth. Despite her efforts to pull the towel around the tin cylinders, they both came tumbling out, crashing on the lid of the washer.

"What was that!?" Gwen took several quick steps down the hall. "Are you OK?"

Natalie shook her head in disgust as she replaced the cans. "We seem to have knocked the Goop Off and WD-40 off the shelf."

Gwen scurried around the corner. "What? I couldn't hear you. Are you OK?"

Gwen's concerned look caused a swift shift in Natalie's attitude, from irritation to shame over her own pettiness. "I'm fine. I just knocked over a few cans." Natalie ran her hand over the lid of the new washer. "It doesn't look like it chipped the enamel anywhere, does it?"

"It looks fine. For once, a quality product."

"I bet that water's just about right now," Natalie said as they walked back to the bathroom. "Oh yeah, anyway, getting back to my story about yesterday. I had to sit and grit my teeth while Ballard points out how vulnerable I am. Being a woman on my own and all."

"It's completely out of some people's frame of reference." Gwen ran her hand through the water. "This should be fine. Where'd you last see Rowdy?"

"She was on the living room windowsill when we started."

"If she doesn't suspect anything, she's probably still there sunning herself."

The two went to the window. Nothing but the tell-tale sign of mussed curtains remained.

"Uh oh. She's wise to us." Natalie peaked under the couch. "I guess what bothers me so much about the thing that Ballard said is…I feel like it's a no-win situation. I mean, on the one hand, straight people bitch that gays are always talking about being gay. Always throwing it in their faces."

"Oh, yeah," Gwen agreed. "There's always that little housewife who grabs the mike during the last rolling credits of Phil Donahue and says something profound like, 'I don't go around telling everybody I'm straight. Why do gay people go around telling everybody they're gay?' Then the show ends with the thunderous approving applause of the audience."

"You're dating yourself with Donahue, but I get your point. This same woman will go to work Monday morning and tell coworkers, 'My husband and I went shopping for furniture this weekend' or 'My husband and I took the kids…'"

Gwen quietly crept to the coat closet, noting that the door was left ajar. She pulled the door open. Her expression of superiority changed to disappointment as her eyes, jetting from corner to corner, found nothing.

Natalie continued. "Could you imagine the look on that same woman's face if I came to work on Monday morning and said, 'My lover and I were shopping for furniture this weekend' or "My lover and I took the kids…"

"Kids?" Gwen mumbled. "At this point, we can't keep track of the cat." She released a sigh of exasperation as she scanned the room

*Information and Belief*

for clues. "Besides, I think the word 'lover' freaks straight people out. They picture the whole relationship as something sexual."

"If you really want to watch 'em freak, let me introduce you as my wife one time."

Gwen laughed. "God! Could you imagine…"

Natalie cut her short with a motion of her hand, her eyes locked on the top of the bookshelf. She stepped lightly as she pointed to the tip of a white tail that hung over the side. Gwen quietly positioned a chair and snatched up the unsuspecting animal. She held the twisting feline over her head in victory. "Gotcha."

"We've degenerated to an all-new low," Natalie teased as they headed back to the bathroom. "We're actually proud of the fact that we outsmarted the cat."

Gwen stroked Rowdy. Slowly, she could feel the fight leave the animal. "Shhh, that's right. Don't listen to the evil mommy. She knows nothing."

"Sometimes I think people are just goading me. I mean, I don't wear a sign or anything. But I don't go out of my way to hide being a lesbian, either. It's not like I've ever made up some phony boyfriend. I talk about you all the time. I just use a more neutral term, like roommate."

Gwen, followed closely by Natalie, took the cat to the bathroom. "Roommate. You're not exactly outing yourself with that."

"Oh, please. You'd have to be mighty naive to think the single woman in your office who always talks about her roommate and has never once mentioned a man is just living with her friend to share expenses. I'm not some kid fresh out of school who just started her first job. Besides, I have a rainbow sticker on my car and, frankly, I look like a lesbian."

Gwen laughed. "You don't look like a lesbian."

"Oh please! I have a lifetime of my mother's observations as evidence." Natalie placed her index finger to her teeth. Gwen began to laugh in anticipation of Natalie's impending impersonation of her mother, as both knew this was her mother's favorite posture when she was about to deliver a line capable of complete destruction of the soul, in what she considered a tactful way. "Dear, don't you think you should wear a little lipstick? It's OK to let people know you're a lady." Natalie shifted her weight to the other foot, switching index fingers. "That's a nice outfit...if you're going for that athletic look. But what are you going to wear tonight?" She shifted back to her original position. "You take such long steps. What's the hurry?"

"You don't look gay," Gwen reassured. "Your mother, somewhere inside herself, knew you were gay. Not because you looked that way, but because she's your mother...and they just know. She told you those things because she thought she could change what was going on inside you by changing the outside."

Natalie sat on the edge of the tub and nodded. "Owwww, you're good. You definitely went into the wrong line of work." She poured the shampoo into her hands, rubbing until a bubbly lather oozed through her fingers. "As for me...professional cat groomer. That was my God-given calling."

"Here you go, baby," Gwen said softly as she lowered the cat toward the water. The animal twisted and wailed in distress. "OK, lather her up."

Natalie bobbed from side to side in a feeble attempt to get around Gwen's body and to the elusive cat. "Think you're smart, huh?" she mocked. She placed one hand on the side ledge of the tub, and pushed tightly to the wall for support. Then, stretching out as far as her small frame would allow, she placed the other hand on the far side. She looked down on the now helpless creature below, let go of the far side, balanced herself, and reached down and started scrubbing in soap with the free hand.

"If ever there was a true Kodak moment. You should see yourself."

"More shampoo," Natalie instructed, holding out her palm.

Gwen eyed Rowdy tentatively. The animal was momentarily still and sullen. "That's a good girl," she quietly praised as she slowly released her grip with one hand to get the bottle. She briefly allowed the newly freed hand to hover, testing the animal's intentions. "That's it." She squeezed the bottle. A fresh stream of liquid spattered out.

Rowdy, startled by the noise and sensing her opportunity, made her break. Gwen dropped the plastic container and lunged to regain her grip. Natalie, shifting her precarious position to assist, felt her slippery hands fumble futilely for a grip on the porcelain as she splashed sideways into the lukewarm water.

"Damn it!!" Natalie yelled.

"Are you OK?" Gwen made every effort to look concerned, but burst into laughter before Natalie could respond.

"Thanks," Natalie said sarcastically. She slowly stood in the tub, looking down at her submerged sneakers. "That's it. We're gettin' a dog."

"Ladies and gentlemen," Gwen announced in grand fashion, "the winner of tonight's wet tee shirt contest."

Natalie quickly snatched the arm extended before her with one hand, pulling Gwen close to her face.

Gwen laughed again. "I thought you were going to pull me in for a second."

"Would I do that?" Natalie said innocently as she lightly kissed her. As Gwen leaned forward to reciprocate, Natalie calmly flipped the water flow lever to the shower position and turned the cold water on.

Gwen screamed and tried to retreat from the wave of ice cold water that poured over her neck and shoulders. Natalie was able to hold her just long enough to drench her head and torso.

"That's not funny," Gwen snapped. "That was really cold."

Natalie, now laughing uncontrollably, stepped out of the tub, her shoes making a squishing sound and losing water from every seam. She sized up Gwen's reaction. The two had been together long enough for Natalie to know the signs. This was a critical moment. Gwen would decide within the next 10 seconds whether to be angry or amused. Natalie raised and lowered her eyebrows a few times. "Taken in by my feminine wiles, eh?"

Gwen, still stinging from the cold blast, began to smile in spite of herself. She wanted to be angry, but she knew the battle was already lost. "According to your mother, feminine wiles would require more make-up and shorter steps," she mocked.

Natalie pulled a clean towel from the rack and put it around Gwen, letting her hands rest on her shoulders. She kissed her lightly. A familiar feeling arose. Great and horrifying. Combat between desire and insecurity. Then, the response. A kiss returned, with the force that wiped out the feelings of inadequacy developed over the course of a lifetime. A kiss that ensured, among other things, that the cat's bath was going to have to wait.

# Chapter 24

Natalie glanced at her watch as the copier pumped out copies of AA/NA sign-in sheets, No-show warning letters, and a number of other miscellaneous forms she kept in her desk. Nine-fifteen. Her pre-sentence interview was late. Not surprising, considering that it was a drug charge. She knew she should be grateful if the zombie found the building. She took her copies, grabbed the fresh stack of memos from her box, and returned to her desk.

The first memo was generated from the office manager. A reminder that the exterminator would be in to spray at the end of the week. "Please remove all objects from the floor that border the wall as that will be the focal point of the spraying." She now knew more about pest control than she had ever really wanted to. She made the notation on her desk calendar, threw the memo away, and moved on.

The second memo was from the deputy director. "Effective immediately, the supervision standard regarding drug testing has been adjusted as follows. In all cases where the probation order reads 'Random drug testing at the discretion of the probation officer,' this testing will be carried out in the following frequency. Two tests per month, until a pattern of four consecutive negative findings has been established, then once monthly for the next six months. If, at this point, all tests are negative, further testing will be at the probation officer's discretion. If, at any time in the process, the probationer tests positive, the agent will make an appropriate response and the process will revert back to bi-weekly testing.

"What?" Natalie said with dismay.

"What?" Bradner echoed.

"Sorry. Just thinking out loud."

"And that was the best you could do," Wood laughed.

She laughed along with him. "That's the best I could do with this new drug testing policy."

"Yeah, I love it when someone tells me what my discretion is," Crew piped in from his side of the divider.

"And what do we do with the people classified as minimum?" Bradner asked. "They're only supposed to report once a month. But now, if they have to drop, they have to come in twice a month."

"Doubling our work," Wood added bitterly.

"Do you suppose they'll double our caseload credit so we can carry half as many bodies?"

"Yeah, right." Wood tossed his pen on his desk in disgust. "You know, one of the things I do to motivate my guys is to remind them that when they've gone a year or so without any trouble, I can reduce their case to minimum supervision and they'll only need to come in once a month. So what do I say now?"

"I don't say anything," Green snapped, turning her chair to join the conversation. "They're all just a bunch of criminals anyway. I don't waste my time explaining anything. They come when I tell 'em. That's it!"

"Oh come on," Wood admonished her. "That attitude doesn't help the young brothers coming in here..."

Excuse me?! My brothers don't come in here. I don't have any brothers. I don't go for all that jive talk. Second, where do you get all this 'help' stuff? We're here to make sure these guys do what they're supposed to do. We're not their social workers."

"And what is it exactly that they're supposed to be doing? Working? Rebuilding their lives?" Wood looked at his desk, sorting papers in no particular order to mask the anger building within him. "And, as for the brother reference, it's not jive talk. If more adult black men and women felt and acted on a kinship..."

"What's any of this got to do with bein' black?" Green shot back. "I'll have you know that most of my caseload is white. So that tells me that we're doin' OK. In the Downriver area, anyway."

"I'm not sure if that's the conclusion you should draw," Natalie added. "We do a lot of pre-sentence reports on young black kids. We just don't get them back for supervision after sentencing."

"That's right," Wood exclaimed, pointing at Natalie and nodding vigorously in agreement.

"So, what does that mean?" Green asked dismissively.

"If the judges aren't sending them back for supervision, then where do you think they're going?" Natalie asked.

Green threw her hands in the air in frustration. "Well, I don't know what you two are talkin' 'bout. All mine come back." She abruptly rose, grabbed a file from her desk, and marched out of the room.

"That's one way," Wood muttered.

"One way?" Natalie repeated.

"Yeah. That's one way to solve a problem. Just ignore the evidence. Deny its existence."

"It's a time honored tradition in my family," Natalie laughed.

"I'm laughing with ya," Wood said with a smile, "but I sure don't think it's funny."

"Neither do I," she agreed.

They were interrupted by the scratchy sound of static feedback from the ailing intercom. "Mr. Wood and Ms. Keller, you have clients."

Natalie looked at her watch: 10:10. "Damn!"

"What are you swearing at? I'm the one with the client," Wood laughed as he restacked the papers he had sorted only moments before, tossing them on top of his filing cabinet.

"I was supposed to have an interview at 9." She set the memos aside and opened the file. She dialed the home phone. It rang four times before being answered by a staunch female voice.

"Good morning," Natalie said. "This is Ms. Fisher with the Probation Department. Is Mr. Alan Chemilewski in?"

"No."

Natalie paused, giving the woman an opportunity to expand on her response. When it became evident that this wasn't going to happen, she continued. "He was scheduled to be here for a pre-sentence interview at 9 a.m. Do you know if he's on his way here ma'am?"

"I doubt it. He's in jail."

"In jail? Do you know which jail he's being held in, ma'am?"

"Old County, over by the Frank Murphy Building."

Natalie's heart sank. She had done a few interviews at the old jail, and had also heard horror stories about it from other agents. She had one last hope. "Do you know what charge he's being held on?"

"Look!" the woman barked. "You're the people who put him there. If you don't know why, then why the hell are you asking me?!"

Before Natalie could begin to explain the separation of the various departments of state, not that she felt this woman really wanted to hear it, she heard the familiar snap and dial tone that had ended a good many of her conversations since she began working for the State.

"Ohhhh, I've got such a bad feeling about this," she mumbled as she dialed the county jail.

The phone rang 13 times before a harried voice answered. "County Sheriff's Department."

"Hi," Natalie said brightly. "This is Ms. Fisher with the Probation Department. I'm calling to check the status of an inmate."

She heard the tapping sound of fingers striking keyboard. A sigh. Then, "Last name."

"Chemilewski. Spelling, C-h-e-m-i-l-e-w-s-k-i."

More tapping. The rhythm matching that of a hunt-and-peck typist. "First and middle initial."

"Alan. He's spelling that with two As and one L."

A pause. "Yeah, he's here. What do you need to know?"

"Estimated out date, and what he's being held on."

Another sigh. "Just a minute. That's on the other screen."

Natalie winced as she looked at her watch again. She felt her anxiety escalate. She had an afternoon interview on the other side of the county.

"No out date. He's being held for 36th district on one count of retail fraud and one count of kidnapping."

Natalie's heart sank. If he was being held on the case she was assigned to investigate, it would have been transferred to the unit located downtown, just 100 yards from the jail. But, due to some politicking on the part of a more forceful office manager at court services, if the prisoner had bonded on his original charge, the case would be assigned to the district office located nearest to the defendant's home. The fact that he was residing in the jail, 100 yards from them and 22 miles from the district office, was insignificant.

Natalie turned off her computer and stuffed the file into her overburdened knapsack.

"We're hitting the field a little early today," Keller observed. "Must be a really good guest on the Rosie O'Donnell show."

Natalie displayed an obligatory smile to the bull pen code for cutting out early. Its origin came from stories from senior agents working half days and 'disappearing' into the field. Those were the days when the county ran probation. Officers were appointed as a political favor, and expectations were low. But when the state took over felony probation, they created a monster known as the audit.

This being a knee-jerk reaction to the few notorious slackers in the system. Once a year, at incredible expense to the state, a bean counter tallied the days between home calls, drug screens, and every other variable on a defendant's court order. And God help the agent who thought that a month meant a calendar month instead of the state's definition of 30 days exactly. And, in true department fashion, the definition of a month was publicized only weeks before the audit, but applied for the entire audit year. The fallout being, an agent's week typically included 40 hours plus an occasional pre-sentence report being dictated at home on a rainy weekend. No overtime or comp time allowed. Junior agents referred to the audits as biblical retribution for "the sins of the father."

## Chapter 25

Natalie squinted against the glare as she glanced from side to side before dashing across Clinton Street. As she had feared, the defendant was being held in the old jail. This was consistent with the way her luck had been running for the past few weeks. She thought back fondly on past interviews in the new jail, and the William Dickerson Facility. The new jail, as it was referred to, was across the street from the Frank Murphy Hall of Justice. The interview rooms had sturdy glass dividers, and deputies who monitored the conversations at all times. And, although the Dickerson Facility didn't have glass dividers, the rooms were large and bright, with easily accessible panic buttons. Then there was the old County Jail. Natalie had often imagined that representatives from third world countries would leave this facility in disgust, run back to the UN, and accuse the city of Detroit of human rights violations.

She pulled the heavy glass door and, upon entry, was grateful that she had opted to skip lunch. Her senses were assailed by a smell that she was sure contained, but was not limited to, urine, vomit, sweat, mold, and just enough disinfectant to give the false illusion that someone cleaned occasionally. She approached the desk. A phone was ringing. The deputy behind the desk ignored both Natalie and the telephone as she maintained a myopic focus on the form before her. She was slumped over, her nose inches away from what seemed to be the center of her universe.

Natalie took the blue pad from the counter and filled out the inmate information. She checked the current inmate list, noting the floor, cell, and bed number of her defendant. Floor 5, cell 1, bed 2. When she completed the form, she placed it, along with her badge, on the counter. She complied with the unstated rule: Don't bother or rush the deputy. That is, unless you don't want them to rush to you when there's a crisis.

Natalie waited quietly. She sensed that the deputy knew she was done. Was even done herself. But both were confined to the custom. After two minutes of silence the deputy got up and, without ever looking directly at Natalie, approved her visit and pointed toward the corridor.

She was greeted at the second security point by the deputy at the metal detector. "Any cigarettes, lighters, or weapons?"

"None," Natalie replied.

He motioned her around the metal detector. This was a good sign. It meant that she hadn't ruffled any feathers thus far. If she had angered anyone, she would have been put through the detector. That was the unspoken way of letting the agent know whether they were going to be treated either like the public, or like a fellow law enforcement officer. "Follow the red line on the floor to the elevator," he instructed as he pointed to the worn red spots that once must had formed a line on the gray floor.

She followed the disjointed markings around the corner, past the freight elevator that she had almost mistakenly taken on her first visit, and around another corner to the passenger elevator. She felt especially tense in this part of the building. It was quiet and isolated. She had originally imagined that a visitor to a jail would be escorted by guards everywhere they went. But she had soon learned that the best she could hope for was a point in the right direction and a grunt from the deputy.

The elevator door opened, and she saw that one deputy and two inmates, clad in orange jump suits, were already inside. She stepped aboard.

The deputy gave a nod and a smile. "Which floor?"

"Five."

"That looks like a probation file," he observed. "Here for a pre-sentence interview?"

"Yeah."

"Who?"

She glanced at the file. "Chemilewski, Alan."

She was startled by the sudden eruption of laughter behind her.

"That's enough," the deputy warned, in a parental tone.

"Fuckin' punk," the tall one mumbled.

"Watch your mouth now, we're in the presence of a lady," the other said mockingly.

The doors opened to her floor. "Hey, tell the lil' ski that Clarence said hi."

"You can also tell him that Clarence won't be eatin' any commissary for the next few days," the deputy shot back.

*Information and Belief*

"Awww, dep," he protested as the door closed.

She stood for a moment in the antechamber, listening to the muffled shouts from the other side of the heavy metal door that separated her from the cell block. She pushed the buzzer and watched the small glass window for signs of life. When the left half of a face appeared in the opening, she pushed her blue pass halfway through the mail slot. It was snatched away. Moments later, several loud metal clanking sounds preceded the opening of the door.

She was led, to her silent relief, to an interview cell. Occasionally, agents were forced to conduct these interviews in the inmate's own cell if an interview cell was not available. Conducting an interview in an inmate cell is complicated by the fact that the other inmates can hear the entire conversation. This forces the inmate into a position of posturing in order to save face in front of his peers.

She entered the cell. The clank of the engaging lock echoed in her ears, along with the typical instruction. "Sit tight. I'll bring him around as soon as I can get to it."

She had wondered what the exact dimensions of the cell were. She knew that from side to side, and front to back, she could touch either wall if she extended both arms. Before each interview, she would tell herself that she was going to measure her own arm span as soon as she got home. But the idea seemed to dissipate as soon as untainted oxygen was allowed to feed her brain.

Two small benches, separated by a table just large enough to hold her file, protruded, seemingly unsupported, from the concrete wall. She often wondered if the walls were gray or a bleached shade of green. The light, which had decreased steadily as she passed from chamber to chamber, was too weak to enable certain identification.

She chose, as always, the bench closest to the bars. She attempted to convince herself that this was a good safety precaution, as it put her about two steps closer to help. She tried to stifle the voice of reality in her head that said, in all likelihood, the deputy would be occupied elsewhere when needed. They don't "hand hold" on professional visits.

She noted the bloody spit on the floor and bars, and considered it to be a concrete reminder that the rules of the interview shift significantly from the office to the cell. This is no place to attempt to establish an authoritarian role. On the other hand, she knew of agents who would request a chair and sit on the outside of the bars. She felt that, although safer in the short run, it showed a level of intimidation that could be used by the perpetrator later. In this situation, she was most comfortable with a more approachable demeanor, focusing more on rapport building.

She reconstructed the questionnaire to her usual order while she waited. The noise level in the professional interview cells was tolerable, as they were separated by several steel doors and at least one antechamber from the cell block.

This was taking even longer than usual. She let the conversation in the next cell substitute for a waiting room magazine.

"Mr. Hewett, my name is Steven Appendamn. I've been assigned to represent you at the pre-trial scheduled to go sometime this afternoon in Judge Ash's court." The sound of rattling papers. "You were bound over from Westland District Court. Is that right?"

"Yeah, but we ain't got time to be talkin' dis shit, man. I didn' do shit. You gotta get me out."

"I'll do everything I can," Appendamn responded in a tone devoid of sincerity.

"Everythin' my ass. I been here six days. I go to court in an hour an dis is da first I see of you. Where the..."

"Listen up," Appendamn interrupted sharply. "I'd be more than happy to go tell the judge that you want one of the other court-appointed lawyers who're sitting on their dead asses in some restaurant in Greektown right about now. You've been in this system long enough to know that this ain't Perry Mason kind of stuff. You sell two rocks of cocaine to an undercover cop and there's just not a big need for an extensive investigation."

The clanking sound of the cell door disengaging brought her mind back to the task at hand. She turned to see the deputy escorting a white male of average build and height to the door. The officer didn't lose a step as he fluidly pointed the man toward the empty bench and continued down the hall, giving a nod over his shoulder to signal that the cell could be closed. The door slammed, the lock engaged, and Natalie detected one of the most foul odors she had encountered in all of her days in the jail. She thought, then quickly dismissed, using an ice-breaking line such as 'Pardon me sir, but do you happen to have a dead rat in your pocket?'

"Boy, am I glad to see you," Chemilewski said eagerly as he sat on the bench. He placed his arms on the table and leaned forward. "No one tells me shit in here."

Natalie paused. She was unaccustomed to being greeted with such enthusiasm. "Mr. Chemilewski, My name is Natalie Fisher and I'm with the probation department. I'm here to…"

"Probation!" he interrupted. Great! That's just great! I thought you were my lawyer."

"I'm afraid not, sir. I'm here to get information from you for a report to the court on your…" She posed, pointing at the file he had pinned under his arms. "I'll need you to lean back, sir."

"Oh, sorry," he said with a laugh. "It's kind of cramped in here."

"Yes it is," Natalie agreed, quietly relieved that his mood seemed to be shifting in a positive direction.

He laughed again. "That's funny. What's that from? Isn't it a beer commercial or something?" He sat up straight and adjusted a non-existent necktie. "Yes, I am!" he imitated. "Which beer commercial is that?"

*Here it is*, she thought. *The stall. These guys get a visit once in a blue moon and they're determined to milk it for all it's worth.* She opened the now-released file. "I'm really not sure, sir. I don't watch much TV." She checked the conviction and referral slip. "I'm here to do the report and sentencing recommendation on your 'attempt possession of less than 25 grams of cocaine' case."

"What do we gotta do that for? I got probation for that."

"No, sir. Your case was referred to probation. They do that every time a person in the state is convicted of a felony. We do a report about your social and legal background and send that along with a sentencing recommendation to the judge."

"My lawyer said I'd get probation," he said defensively.

"And you probably will," she agreed. "Attempt possession in Wayne County will usually get you probation. But I never make guarantees. Judges can and will do just about anything they want."

"So, what about my other case?" he asked as he leaned forward onto the small surface, again covering her file.

Natalie leaned back, attempting to make the move look casual and not the knee-jerk reaction to the combination of his closeness and the sickening smell of his breath. She pointed to her file. He quickly took his arms off the document. His immediate and startled reaction to her gesture told her that he was either new to the criminal justice system, or trying to impress her. Either way, it was a welcome response.

She opened the file, removing the printout she had run on the court computer across the street, on her way to the jail. "It looks like you're scheduled for arraignment on kidnapping and retail fraud next week, out of the 36th District Court. Technically, that's why you're being held. Your lawyer was smart enough to bond you on my case right away."

"What's the difference. In jail is in jail. Right?"

"Not really. You see, the odds are, if you're convicted on the kidnapping, even with a good plea to a lesser charge, you're going to get some jail time. But usually, the judge won't give you any time on a possession charge. So you'll get credit for time served on the only charge that you're likely to get time for. Do you see what I mean?"

He sat back, crossing his arms. "Who's on first?"

She smiled, immediately recognizing the old Abbott and Costello bit. "That's right. Who is on first." She clicked her pen and leaned toward the page. The small print and the dim lighting were a poor combination. She wondered if the people who put the packet together ever considered the conditions under which it would be used. Then she remembered. They didn't care.

"You know," he said, "before we get started, I just want you to know I'm not some crazed kidnapper or something. It's not like I went and grabbed a kid off the playground or took hostages or anything."

"Well sir, I'm really not here about that anyway, and..."

He waved his hands and let out a sigh, releasing an odor that tested the limits of her gag reflex. "I know. I know. You're here on the other thing. But, you gotta be thinkin', 'What kind of crazy criminal am I dealin' with.' Well, it's not like that."

Natalie sat back from the page. She had seen this brand of determination before. There was no stopping this story. She might as well lean back and get as far away from the accompanying stench as possible.

"You see, it all started when I owed this guy some money for some stuff he'd fronted me. It's not like I was workin' or anything, so gettin' up his money was tough. Anyway, guys like that, they don't like to wait for what's theirs. So they start makin' threats. Now, don't get me wrong. I could handle anything they might have been thinkin' of doin' to me. But, they knew where my mom lived. And I was afraid for her. Not for me. Anyway, I decide I'm gonna do what I gotta do. I go to the Super K and I fill a cart with about six or seven VCRs. I pick VCRs because they're easy to sell and they're light. Easy to run off with in a hurry."

"High profit and low liability," Natalie said with a shrug. "Makes sense so far. You should have considered a career in business management." She glanced at her watch. "We really need to get on with the interview for this case, sir. I've got to be on the other side of the county in about an hour, and..."

"I'm almost done," he interrupted. "So, I bolt out of the store with the cart and the VCRs. Usually, this works. It's so...so...I don't know...so in your face, nobody does nothin'. They all look at each other, like 'Did you see that?' They don't do nothin'. But this time, two guys come flyin' out right after me. And I'm thinkin' what the hell are these guys doin'? So I leave the cart about half way 'cross the lot and I keep goin'. But that's just not good enough for our two super heroes. They gotta run by the cart and keep comin' after me. So I get about a block. Now, I'm not in the shape I used to be. You know, the drugs and all. So I start lookin' for anything. Then I see her."

He stopped. Natalie looked at her watch again. There was no way out. "You saw who?"

"My mom. She was sittin' in her car at the gas station. I mean, life doesn't get any better than that. Right?" He looked at her, waiting for some acknowledgment of his truth. Although he got none, he continued. "So I get in her car and I yell, 'Drive, damn it, drive!' Now, it's not like I usually yell at my mother. But I sure didn't want her to get in trouble. So I keep yellin', 'Drive, damn it. Drive!'" He paused. "Then I looked. Then I looked again. And it wasn't my mother at all. Just some lady lookin' like she's about to shit. So I'm thinkin' Oh shit. What do I do now? So then I think, it won't do your mother any good if you get caught. So, even though I know that it's not her, I keep yellin' at her to drive. When she don't, I reach in my jacket and act like I got a gun or somethin' in my pocket and I say,

'Don't make me hurt you lady. Just drive. That's all you gotta do.' So, she does. I get out after a few blocks and walk home. I no sooner get in the front door when two cops jump on me. No warning or nothin'. Just jump on me and slap cuffs on my wrists so tight that my hands turn blue. My poor mother was just standin' there cryin' and they didn't even care."

"How did they know where to look?" Natalie asked.

"I guess one of the guys remembered me. I used to work there."

Natalie closed her eyes, exhaled, and rubbed the back of her neck. She looked up and met the expectant gaze of this childlike man, waiting for her approval. "So what you're telling me is, you did it all for your mother."

"Yeah. That's right. What else could I do?"

A part of her wanted to scream. Grab him by the collar, pull his smelly face close to her, slap him up side his silly head and say, "Who the hell are you kidding? You pulled the same scam you've pulled a dozen times before. You did it because you wanted what you wanted right now, instead of working for it. You wanted your drugs, and the last thing that was on your selfish little mind was your mother. Odds are, you've ripped her off in one way or another so many times that she keeps everything she hold dear under lock and key for fear that you'll sell it for chump change."

The other part of her knew that he wouldn't hear a word of it, and would probably pummel her beyond recognition before a deputy would consider coming to investigate the sound of the screams. In his mind, she'd become another one of the unreasoning masses who had it in for him.

She leaned over the form, shifting as close to the wall as the small bench would allow to let the slightly improved hall light hit the paper. "Please give me the correct spelling of your last name."

## Chapter 26

Natalie turned the heater fan off and opened her jacket while merging from I-375 to I-75 South. The contrast between the chilly three-block run from the jail, to the heat created by a sun magnified by glass and thrown against the dark interior of her car, sent her from chills to sweats in a matter of minutes. The unpredictability of her days made wardrobe selection a game of Russian roulette with a fully loaded revolver. However, if the stories of "the good ol' days" of probation could be believed, she could consider herself lucky in many respects. The Probation Department was once a county-run program located on the 11th floor of the Old Recorder's Court Building. The first and foremost complaint with this setup was that the elevator only ran to the 10th floor. From there, visitors had to be directed down several halls and up a flight of stairs. There were six agents accommodated in one large room, and they shared the floor with the Psych clinic. This lead to more than one interview being interrupted by a sudden, blood curdling scream. However, as the Psych clinic often registered the same complaint regarding the unexpected outbursts of the probationers, an eventual peace was negotiated. On one occasion, the two staffs overheard the excited chatter of the court deputies, revealing that a bomb threat had been called in the previous day and the entire building, with the notable exception of the forgotten 11th floor, had been evacuated. From that day forward, a bond was firmly established between the two departments.

Natalie drove slowly down one of the many segmented, numerically-named streets of Wyandotte. She glanced at her notes and back to the houses. She had been delayed another 10 minutes by a train. Natalie was convinced the name of the city, Wyandotte, was a Native American word for 'City Divided by Train Tracks.'

She stopped in front of an old, well-maintained colonial. She shut off the engine, closed her eyes, and took several slow, deep breaths, exhaling in a methodical fashion. She rolled her shoulders a few times, then opened her eyes. She found this to be the best stress-reducing technique that time and space allowed while in the field.

She realized that if she didn't take the time to pull herself back in, her letters and numbers would suffer. The logical side of her mind knew that having dyslexia was nothing to be ashamed of. But, since she didn't wear a sign that said "dyslexic," she was pretty sure that most people still thought she was just plain stupid every time she forgot how to spell a simple word. Gwen had spent a lot of time working with her, reading and implementing new techniques. Some of it had helped. Even if it didn't eliminate the problem, it normalized the experience. But 12 years of laughing peers, and teachers who rolled their eyes and attributed the problem to poor study habits, often within earshot of those same peers, would take a long time to overcome.

Her finger pushed the door bell simultaneously to the opening of the door.

"Good afternoon. You must be Miss Fisher," the gray-haired woman said warmly. "I was so afraid that I had the wrong day."

"No ma'am," Natalie replied sheepishly. "I apologize. I got held up down at the..."

"No need to apologize, dear," she replied in an amiable tone as she lead Natalie through a clean, formal looking living room to the kitchen. "I hope you'll excuse the mess. I can't spend the time on the chores that I used to. I had to take a part-time job to help Eric with his legal fees."

Natalie scanned the kitchen. It was immaculate.

"Can I get you something? A coffee or a Coke, maybe?"

"No thank you ma'am," Natalie answered warmly as she sat. She liked this woman. She reminded Natalie of her own grandmother, and the weekends spent at her home on the lake. A never-ending supply of soda pop and candy usually preceded the rides in her motor boat. She felt a surge of excitement as she recalled the feeling of the wind rushing through her hair and the pitch of the boat against the wake. "Where are you working?"

"I'm a greeter at the Meijer store," she replied with a sigh.

"It doesn't sound like you care much for that." Natalie opened her file. She had the workbook open to the marriage and family section.

"Oh, it's not the job, I guess. It's just me. I haven't worked since my firstborn. Things have changed." She looked off into the distance, and for a moment Natalie wondered if she remembered that she was there. "People have changed," she continued. "They don't meet your eyes when you say hello. They just speed right by. I know it sounds silly...but it makes me feel...I don't know...it makes me feel...dirty, when they don't want to look at me. They pretend that they don't hear me. Like they don't know I'm talking to them."

Natalie felt a jolt of shame as she thought about all the times she blew right by store greeters. It had never occurred to her that they would care one way or the other. She resisted the urge to apologize for herself, and all the selfish people like her, who wanted nothing more than that quick can of cat food on the way home.

The woman laughed. "I'm sorry. Once I get started. Well...I'm sure this isn't what you drove all the way over here to talk about."

"No problem," Natalie assured as she glanced to the table at the open file. "First, I just need to verify some basic stuff. Your name is Alice Newkirk, is that right?"

"That's right. Alice Lee Newkirk," she confirmed.

"You are 61 years old and reside here."

"That's right."

"Eric's mother's name is Janet Alton. She's 40 years of age and lives in Trenton with her husband, Eric's stepfather, David Alton. Is that right?"

She sighed. "That's right. Eric's mother is my eldest. I love her, but I just can't go along with the way she's treated Eric."

"And how is that?" Natalie prompted.

"First, it was the drinking." She looked at the table mat and ran her finger along the floral pattern. The lines seemed to deepen in her face. "It started in her early teens. I didn't know it at the time. But years later...well...you know how things come out in angry outbursts. People blame."

"She blamed you," Natalie said softly.

"She blamed everyone. Me she blames for...I don't know...for being around too much when she didn't want me and not enough when she did. She blamed her father for working himself to death." She stopped, her eyes rolling toward the ceiling. "He died of a massive heart attack the year after Daniel was born." Her eyes went back to the mat. "She blamed school for being too hard." She stopped, seemingly lost in her own thoughts. "Then came the boys. They called at all hours, came at all hours. She started to stay out later, go to school less." She looked up from the mat and met Natalie's eyes. "Do you have children?" she asked softly.

After a fleeting moment of indecision, Natalie decided to answer. The flow of the interview was going far too well to play it cagey. "No."

"There's not another feeling in the world like watching your child fall apart before your very eyes." Alice went back to her pattern tracing. This time pushing her fingernail into the plastic, creating a ridge that deepened with every pass. "She got pregnant, had Eric. At first she was excited about having a baby. She got a lot of attention from her girlfriends. They'd come over for an hour or two and play with him like a doll. But then they'd go. She'd get moody because she couldn't go too. Then she had someone new to blame. Eric. She'd fly off the handle. Scream at him over every little thing. When I'd try to calm her down, she'd scream at me, storm out, and stay gone for days at a time. Sometimes she'd come home drunk. Once, she even came home all beat up."

"How long did this cycle last?" Natalie asked as she scribbled frantically to keep up.

"Until she met Eric's step-father." Alice sighed and shook her head. "At first, I thought he would be just what she needed. He came straight out the first time he met me and said he was an alcoholic, but he'd been sober for over three years. From that night on, Janet went six months and never touched a drop. They got married and took Eric to their new home. That was real hard for me. By that time, it felt like Eric was my own. But I knew deep down that a child belongs with his mother, so I put on a brave front. I could see a little bit of the fear in Eric's eyes too. But then, we just looked at each other…without sayin' a word…we just both knew this was the way it had to be. We've always had that kind of link, he and I."

"What brought him back here?"

"One day, about four months later, I got a call from a social worker at the youth home in Detroit. Janet had taken Eric there about a week before and said she just couldn't control him. She was pregnant with her second child by then. She told them that Eric was a mean boy and she was afraid to have him 'round the new baby."

"Had you seen any signs of anti-social behavior when he was with you?"

She paused. When she looked up from the mat Natalie could see that she was fighting back tears. "He was never a mean boy. He wasn't a bad boy. It was that husband of hers. He wanted his own little family. Eric would never be a part of that. Janet had a choice to make, and she made it." She rose abruptly and went to the cupboard. "Are you sure you won't have a cup of coffee?"

"No thank you."

Mrs. Walker poured a cup, carefully placed it in the matching saucer, and returned to the table. "It's just too easy to get rid of children," she continued bitterly. "She just went to court and told some judge that she couldn't control him. There was some legal word for it. But I just can't remember."

After an uncomfortable silence, Natalie decided to fill in the blank. It was a term that had come up in child welfare, her former career, many times. "She filed a petition of incorrigibility?"

"That's it," Mrs. Walker responded quickly. "Incorrigibility," she repeated in a tone that made it sound profane. "It means you can't control your own child. In my day, the shame was on the parent when the child was out of control. Now, they just send 'em away."

"It couldn't have been easy for you," Natalie said sympathetically. "They didn't have a family counseling program on every corner back then."

"To be honest," she replied softly, "I don't think much of those things. Problems should be handled quietly...within the family. Airing your dirty linen in public never cured anything. But I could never convince my daughter of that. You would have thought that having a child out of wedlock was something to be proud of. No amount of talking on my part could get her to do the right thing."

"What is the right thing?"

She sighed. "I know things are different now. But in my day, if a girl got herself in...a family way...she'd go somewhere, have the baby, then come back. If she was careful and kept a tight tongue, she came back with her reputation intact."

"What is their relationship like now?"

She hesitated. "What do you mean?"

"Eric and his mother, I mean. Do they get along? See each other? Visit? How often? That kind of thing."

"Things are better now," she replied quickly. "She gives him money. Invites him to all the holidays and birthdays."

*All the right things*, Natalie thought. "But he still chooses to live here with you," Natalie observed.

"Oh, it's not that they won't have him. I just have more room."

"It is a beautiful house," Natalie said as she put her pen away.

"Why thank you, dear," she beamed. "I've done the best with what I have. Would you like to see the rest of it?" she added eagerly.

"I'd love to." Natalie closed her folder to expedite her departure. It had been her experience that some older folks would keep her half the day if she didn't carefully choose her moment...the slightest pause between sentences...and bolt for the door.

"Come to the second floor. That's what I'm the most proud of," she boasted as they climbed the stairs. "This was once divided into two rooms. My kids used to stay up here. When the youngest left, I had most of the wall taken out. It gives it an open, airy look, don't you think?"

"Absolutely," Natalie agreed. The first room had been converted into what seemed to be a huge walk-in cupboard. Shelves were built into every inch of available wall space. And every inch was neatly filled with canning jars with every imaginable vegetable and mixed vegetable combination. The jars were spotless, and arranged artfully by color. "Incredible," she said under her breath as she walked past the half wall. The hardwood floors, unlike the ones she remembered from childhood, were more than a match for her weight, refusing to give up so much as a squeak.

Past the wall, she saw what could only be described as a good likeness of the general store in an old *Waltons* or *Little House on the Prairie* rerun. A counter was covered with big glass jars of hard candies. Antique medicine bottles were displayed in one case, old rifles and hunting knives in another. Tools, obviously old judging by the materials they were made of, but clean and polished enough to be taken for new. Dolls. Some made of porcelain. Others of wood. Still others of fabric, with faces skillfully drawn or sown.

"I've had most of these things for years," the woman said, "just stored in boxes. The fees at those storage places are so steep, I have to admit I seriously thought about selling the whole lot. But the porcelain dolls belonged to my mother. That's just not something you can sell."

"I know Michigan basements are usually a little damp," Natalie said. "But couldn't you have run a dehumidifier or something?"

"All the homes in this neighborhood are slabs. Just a crawl space."

"It's an incredible display." Natalie stared into yet another glass case that contained antique bottles. "These are some heavy duty cases."

"When the Turner jewelry store went out of business I got those for next to nothing."

"Oh, I agree, they're beautiful. But all this weight right over, ah, where would we be right now, right over the kitchen?"

"Oh no dear, my room is under this part of the house. But I'm sure it's quite safe."

"Your room," Natalie laughed. "I must be all turned around. Then what would this counter be over?" she asked as she crossed the room and laid her hand on the smooth oak surface.

"You're over the utility room. I got that counter at an estate auction. And what a deal. I heard about it from a friend that made deliveries to Grosse Ile. Apparently, the newspaper messed up the ad. There must have been fewer than 30 people there."

"Quite a coup." Natalie said as she wandered back toward the canning jars. "My mother took a stab a canning once when I was a kid. I remember that it seemed to take the whole day. Boiling the jars, cooking the veggies and putting the right amount of spices...or...I don't know...would it have been a preservative of some kind? Anyway, I remember waiting to hear those tops pop so she'd know they were sealed. By the time it was over, the kitchen was a million degrees, my mom was exhausted and we had...oh, maybe seven jars of tomatoes."

Mrs. Walker laughed. "It's not that much work. And it is important to can enough at any one time to make it worth while. It sounds like your mother was a city girl."

Natalie laughed. "Good observation." She walked toward the stairs. "OK, I think I've got it now. So, this room must be over the kitchen and the living room."

"Now you've got it," Mrs. Newkirk replied as she led the way down the stairs.

"Yeah, I think I do," Natalie said quietly as she followed. *A one bedroom house with no sign of anyone camping out on a couch*, she thought. *All old lady things. He doesn't live here.*

"I'm sorry, did you say something?" Mrs. Walker asked.

"Oh, just that I thank you for your time. I know it's never easy to open your house to a stranger."

Natalie had her hand on the doorknob when she heard the inevitable question in the soft, tentative voice. "What's next, Miss Fisher? What's going to happen to Eric now?"

"I really can't say," Natalie replied, falling back on her pat response. "I still have to talk to some other people, then I write a report and make a recommendation. But in the end, it's all up to the judge."

"I just don't understand the world today. I mean, as much as I don't approve of sex outside of marriage, a boy can't be expected to ask a girl for her driver's license to check her age, can he?"

"That's really not an issue that I'll be dealing with, ma'am." Natalie looked into the aged eyes that begged for a glimmer of hope. Searched for a sign. "The important thing right now is that he's as honest as he can be with me...about everything."

Natalie saw the rapid transition of expression, from quizzical to realization. And from realization to shame. Mrs. Newkirk had lied, and she had been caught.

## Chapter 27

Natalie headed down Fort Street toward Trenton. It was 4:05 p.m. according to the digital clock on her dash. Too late to go back to the office and get started on anything useful, but too early to go home for the day. She opened the file at the next red light and pulled out the police report. She was in luck. She knew that, normally, investigators don't put a juvenile sexual assault victim's address in the report. But in this case, since the incident happened in the girl's home, it had to be in the report to establish jurisdiction of the case.

Natalie was familiar with the complex, as it was the only subsidized housing in the city. It had opened when she was in elementary school. She remembered the kids in her 1st grade class, undoubtedly expressing what they were hearing at home, talk about how "the new people" were going to change things. They said that people were going to have to start locking their houses, and told how their parents had bought them brand new chains and locks for their bikes. When Natalie told her mother this and asked when she was going to get a new chain and lock for her bike, her mother reminded her that she already had one and had been locking her bike up ever since she had been allowed to ride it to school. She said that these new kids were going to be the same as anybody else, and that the people saying these things were just afraid of change. She chose not to use the word bigot until Natalie got older.

Unlike the projects Natalie visited in the larger cities, these buildings were well maintained, and the local schools were some of the best in the state. Natalie had often thought that if she had to be poor, this was the place she'd want to live. Although crime in the complex was proportionally higher than in the rest of the city, there was a strong community group that worked actively to keep drugs and gangs out. She'd felt more of a sense of community there than in her own neighborhood, where she and her neighbors exchanged little more than a polite wave as they bolted from car to house and back each morning and evening.

She parked in the lot in front of Temple Square and made her customary check of her surroundings. Nothing seemed out of place. A young woman walking with an overloaded laundry basket and a child following close behind. A middle-aged black man under the hood of an old Plymouth, elbow high in grease. She looked at the report. Mother, Wanda Jackson. Daughter, Brenda Jackson. *Mother, Wanda. Daughter, Brenda. Jackson. It doesn't mention a father. Better go with Ms.* "Ms. Wanda Jackson," she repeated aloud several times to herself as she approached the door. Natalie felt that the system was rough enough on victims. She considered messing up the name as the ultimate insult.

She heard the canned laugh track of what she assumed to be a mid-day sitcom rerun. The volume of the television reduced significantly as soon as she rang the bell. Experience told her she had about a 70% chance of making contact with anyone. Some would sit quietly until she walked away. Her odds were increased by the fact that this was a victim and a television, as opposed to a felon and a stereo.

With the latter scenario, the door would open about 30% of the time. When it did, usually a full three to five minutes after the third ring of the bell, she would usually be greeted by a smiling red-eyed young man, the overpowering smell of marijuana, and several other young men sitting on a couch, hands in their laps, smiling nervously. The older and wiser felon will, in spite of the fact that he knows you heard him, not answer the door. He has learned that you can't prove what you can't see.

She reached her hand toward the doorbell a second time, but pulled back when she heard light steps approach. The knob slowly turned and the door opened as wide as the fastened chain would allow. Natalie looked down to meet the suspicious gaze of a young girl. She pushed the bangs of her dark brown hair from her eyes. Her hand paused just long enough over her face to give Natalie the impression that she used the gesture regularly in a futile attempt to hide.

"Hi," Natalie greeted in her most non-threatening tone. "Is Ms. Wanda Jackson home?"

The young girl shifted back slightly. "She can't come to the door right now," she said softly. The presentation struck Natalie as the same rehearsed response she got in child welfare from children who were left home alone.

Natalie hesitated. She was always uncomfortable about leaving messages with children. For a moment, she considered that this girl might be the victim. She didn't want to do anything that could even be misinterpreted as an attempt to interview a minor without the parent's consent. However, she dismissed the idea as she recalled the victim's age to be 12 or 13. This girl couldn't be any older than nine. Natalie took her badge case out of her pocket and withdrew a business card.

"Are you a cop?" the girl asked cautiously.

Natalie laughed. "No. I'm a probation officer." She slowly handed the card to the girl through the opening. "Could you give her this and ask her to call me?"

"OK," she replied. She closed the door before Natalie could offer any further explanation.

# Chapter 28

Sophia sat uneasily as she listened to one side of a conversation that she knew would put Eric in a pissy mood.

"Are you sure?" A pause. "But you told her I live there. Right?" Another pause. "The sneaky little bitch!" Followed immediately by "I'm sorry, I'm sorry. I know. That's no way to talk. It's just that...well, are you really sure she knows? Tell me exactly what she said."

Sophia went to the refrigerator and brought Eric a beer. He took the bottle and waved her away. "No, no," he reassured. "It's not your fault. But this just goes to show you what I've said before. You just can't trust these people." Another pause. "I know she sounded really nice. But look what she did. What *they* do. They come to your house and act all nice. But they just use and twist everything."

Eric's tone lowered and Sophia was unable to hear the conversation end.

"What happened?" she asked as he flopped on the couch.

"The sneaky little bitch," he snarled. He tilted the bottle of Budweiser, allowing the perfect mixture of air and gravity combine for the drink to roll smoothly down his throat.

"What happened?" she asked again.

"She got all comfy with her. Then she started snoopin' around. She got Grams so into explainin' everything in the house, that she forgot to save a room for me."

"What do you mean?"

"She got Grams showin' off the house. You know. Like, this is the kitchen, this is the livin' room. So on and so on. By the time she was done, she'd showed her everything and there was no place for me. No room for me."

"Couldn't she have said you were sleeping on the couch or..."

"We went over all that," he interrupted. "She said that there was just this point in their talk when she could tell that she knew. Now she feels bad 'cause this woman thinks she's..." He stopped abruptly and pulled his wallet from his back pocket. "Did that card have a home number on it?" he wondered aloud. "It did. I know it did," he said as he checked and rechecked his billfold. "Did you put that card somewhere?" he asked, as he hurried to the bedroom.

"What are you talking about?" she asked.

"I can still fix this," he said frantically as he rummaged through the change and receipts on his dresser. "What did you do with that card?" he yelled.

"I didn't do anything with any card," she responded defensively. "Besides, I don't think..."

"You don't think...You don't think," he said mockingly as he pushed by her, knocking her to the floor. He snatched his keys from the night stand. "The first fuckin' time you decide to think and you pick now." He stormed toward the door. "You better hope that fucker's in the car. If it ain't, then I know you threw the fucker out."

## Chapter 29

Natalie tossed her keys on the table with one hand while fanning the mail with the other. Consumer's Power, a coupon mailer from the drug store, and the book club. She heard the storm door open, followed by the fumbling of keys. "I've got it," she announced as she crossed the room and pulled the door open. Gwen released her keys, allowing them to swing in the lock as the door opened before her. "You're home early."

Gwen smiled weakly. The emotional toll of the past few weeks had manifested itself in the sapping of her strength. "John and Glen had a meeting in Kalamazoo at 4:30."

"Ouch," Natalie empathized, pulling Gwen's key from the door.

"Bad break for them," she agreed. "But at least I could cut out early." She walked to the refrigerator and added, "I even had a chance to do a little Christmas shopping."

Natalie raised her eyebrows. "For whom?"

"For you," she laughed. "And don't be a snoop."

"Me?" she said innocently. "I'm not snooping." She picked up Gwen's purse. "I'm just being helpful. Putting your keys away. If I should happen to chance upon…"

"There's nothing in there. Nice try."

"OK. That rules out jewelry." She went to the window and drew the curtain aside. "No pony in the driveway. Guess I'm stumped."

"Very funny." Gwen smelled the milk, made a face at its week-old expiration date, and dumped it down the sink.

"I am very funny," Natalie said as she came up behind and slipped her arms around Gwen. She gave a gentle squeeze and rested her head between her shoulder blades. "I'm quite possibly the funniest person you know."

Gwen turned, laced her fingers behind Natalie's neck and gave her a playful peck on the forehead. "If that's the case, I really need to get out more."

"Whew. Please feel free to pull that knife out while you've got your hands back there."

Gwen closed her eyes and pulled Natalie closer. She let out a quiet sigh and allowed herself relax in her arms. "Sorry. I'm just in a really lousy mood." She loosened her grasp and pulled back. "It feels so weird. I was out shopping. Having a really good time. Then I thought about all the people who are going to find out that they're getting the ax tomorrow."

"Tomorrow's the day."

"Yep," she said with a tone of resignation. "I've looked at it from every angle. It seems like I've got it down to letting the fewest people go with the numbers I was given to work with."

"There's not much more you can do."

"It's really ironic. We posted the plant-wide meeting this morning. Just before I left, I heard that the rumor is that we're announcing a Christmas bonus."

"This would have to be the one time the rumor mill gets so far off the track."

"How does pasta sound? I think we still have some frozen sauce from the other night."

"Sure. That's fine," Natalie responded.

"What was your day like?"

"Strange. First I had to go to the old jail. That's always a real treat. I had to sit with a smelly thief and write down his lies and excuses."

"Sounds like a bad start." Gwen unwrapped the frozen sauce and placed the cube in a pan.

Natalie took the packaged noodles out of the cupboard and placed them on the counter. "From there I had to drive down to Wyandotte and interview a sweet grandmother type."

"I'm almost afraid to ask what she did."

"It wasn't her. In this case, the lies and excuses were on behalf of her grandson."

"I'm beginning to think you're becoming jaded." She pushed the melting cube in the sauce pan with a wooden spoon. "How do you know all these people are lying?"

"Well, the first guy claims to have car-jacked a 22-year-old Hispanic woman driving a Corvette because he mistook her for his 55-year-old mother who drives a station wagon."

Gwen laughed. "Sounds like an honest mistake."

"Sure," Natalie agreed. "I mean, once you figure out you've got the wrong person...I guess it would be downright rude to just get out."

"What about the old lady?"

"She was very nice." Natalie took the plates from the cupboard and placed them next to Gwen by the stove. "The house was beautifully maintained. She had some of the most interesting antiques I've ever seen. The problem was that between the parts of the house I'd seen and the parts she described, there was only one bedroom. It was pretty obvious that he wasn't living there."

"Couldn't he be sleeping on the couch?"

"I doubt it. She has it in plastic. I don't think she even lets anyone sit on it, let alone sleep on it." Natalie picked up the phone and began punching in numbers.

"Who are you calling?"

"Just checking my voice mail."

"I'm glad you decided to get that service. I can't believe the state requires you to give your home number to felons."

"The funny thing is, when they got our business cards back from the printer, they were wrapped in clear plastic with the phone number covered on the outside of the plastic wrap in black marker. So I asked the area manager's secretary why the number was blacked out. She explained that she had done it since she was putting them in our mailboxes where anyone could see them."

"So they give your number to every felon on the street, but they're willing to protect you from your fellow agents."

Natalie listened to the beginning of her greeting. "Hello, you have reached..." She pushed the pound button and entered her code. "You have no new messages."

# Chapter 30

Natalie's mailbox was jammed. She grabbed the bundle, swung into the front office to sign in, and went back to the bull pen. Green was already in, but morning chatter wasn't one of her strengths. Not with Natalie, anyway. This suited her this morning. The packed mailbox and repetitive blink of her answering machine were the normal consequence of an afternoon in the field.

As was her custom, Natalie opted to deal with the mail first. Experience had taught her that very few of her felons, no matter how badly they had wanted to talk to her the day before, appreciated a 7:45 a.m. wakeup call. She pulled her two-hole punch from the shelf behind her, and punched and re-filed all the amended orders and discharge copies that had been returned from typing. Then she reviewed all the drug test results. No surprises there. She was getting pretty good at knowing who was going to be dirty and who would be clean before the confirmation arrived. She entered the results in the road notes.

"Can you believe this?" Bradner fumed.

"Good morning. I didn't see you come in." Natalie continued to sort papers, crossing her name off the buck slip on the Avon cover and tossing it to one side.

"I'm sorry. But of all the asinine things this department has ever done, this is…"

"You know what your problem is Ed?" She continued before he could respond. "You start your day with the memos. I like to ease into my day. Here," she said, extending the Avon book to him. "Do a little Christmas shopping."

"Thanks, but I think I'll pass." He gently hung his coat on his side of the divider with one hand while holding the flimsy artificial wall with the other.

Natalie laughed. "It's like working in a house of cards."

He looked at her questioningly. She pointed to the wall. "Oh, yeah," he said. "I guess so. I thought you were talking about the memo. Then I thought, 'Wait a minute, I thought she said she hadn't read that.'"

Natalie laughed again. "Looking for gaps in my story. You've been working here too long."

"Be that as it may, when you read this, I think you'll agree that we've all been working here too long."

Keller walked two steps in the doorway and stopped abruptly. "I just hate when days start like this."

"Start like what?" Crew asked as he stepped around her.

"I'm not exactly sure," she responded. But whenever I enter a room and hear someone questioning their career choice before 8 a.m., I know it's going to be a long day."

"OK. I know you've been busting to tell us." Natalie set the depleted stack of papers aside. "What's in store for us? Memo, Policy Directive, or new Procedure?"

"Memo," Bradner replied. "It's addressed to all area managers. You know what that means."

"That we'll have at least three copies by the end of the day?" Keller guessed.

"Besides that," he conceded.

"It's a nasty-gram. Someone's pissed," Crew concluded.

"You got it," Bradner acknowledged. "And it's none other than the primadonnas of the county…yes, the Recorder's Court Cashiers."

The group let out a collective groan that brought Green scurrying over. "What in the hell do they want now?"

"It must be another CTN scandal," Natalie offered. "Do you remember when they held up all the amended orders because they decided that they needed us to put the criminal tracking number on all the orders?"

"Yeah, they even held up orders that had nothing to do with money, just to make their point," Keller recalled.

"What about the time they sent a month's worth of money orders back because they were stapled with that backdated policy directive?" Crew rubbed his temples. "My phone rang off the hook for a week with victims wanting to know why I didn't send my guys to jail for not paying their restitution."

"Well, the latest and greatest is as follows." Bradner stiffened and cleared his throat to add an air of authority to his words. "This is from our beloved regional manager. 'It has come to my attention that some agents are calling the cashier's department and requesting information regarding the total amount of attorney fees assessed. This practice is to stop immediately. Please be advised that this situation will be monitored. Amended orders that quote the determination of that fee as being due to information received by the Recorder's Court Cashier will be sent to my attention.'"

"That's the stupidest thing I've ever heard!" Green blasted. "So, what they want us to do is get in our car, drive the 20-some odd miles round trip every time a court order sets attorney fees in an amount to be determined. Then they want us to write an amended order to set the amount, and send it to the cashier who already has the amount in the computer sitting in front of her."

"You should never start with the memos," Natalie mumbled as she wandered out, coffee cup in hand. She understood his frustration. It made little sense to drive 22 miles to retrieve information for a person who already had it. But, after all, the state paid for her mileage and her time. Additionally, there were few aspects of her job simpler than writing an amended order. You need only remind the judge of the original condition (attorney fees to be determined), and write a short sentence stating the change that is needed and citing the source of your information (per Recorder's court computer, these fees should be set at $410). Natalie signed as the petitioner, the judge signed it, then it was a new condition of probation. Simple. This particular policy, as wasteful as it was, wasn't costing Natalie a thing. She had learned to give these issues a low priority on her personal frustration scale.

"Beat ya," Moore said with a satisfied smile as he poured his coffee. "The first cup is always the best."

"A great tag line. You should go into advertising." She held out her cup.

"I live to serve," he said with a mock British accent. "Will you require anything else?"

"Cream, sugar and a...please feel free to conduct this morning's interview, and detail my car."

"Sorry ma'am, but I don't do interviews."

"Smart man," Ballard chimed in as she entered. She poured her coffee while Natalie doctored hers with the usual combination of cream and a little more sugar than anyone really needs. "I know I've said this before," Ballard continued, "but yesterday..." she held one hand up in resignation. "Yesterday was truly that one interview too many."

"Oh boy," Moore said with excited anticipation as he pulled out a chair and ushered Ballard to it.

"You're a sick man," she responded with false contempt.

"It's a corrections department tradition," Natalie said in his defense. "If your misfortune can give our day even the slightest levity, you owe it to us. Now spill!"

"OK. Well, yesterday I had this CSC interview. I knew right away that something just wasn't right because this was a CSC 1st degree."

"How does a child rapist get bond?" Moore wondered aloud. "That's an automatic incarceration. His family's either loaded, or..."

"*Or* is the correct answer," Ballard interrupted. "I went to the lobby to get this guy and he's got this kind of blank look when he walks toward me. I guess blank isn't a good description. It was more a dull, expressionless look. Anyway, I see he's got nothing in his hands, so I ask if he brought all the documents on his list. Then this other guy pops up, it ends up to be his brother, and says he has all the stuff. Then he adds that his brother will probably need his help to answer questions. So it seems obvious to me that I'm going to get nowhere fast without this brother. This guy is either slow or autistic or something. So I ask the brother to join us for the interview."

"I hate having family members in an interview," Crew offered, joining them at the table.

"So do I," Ballard agreed. "But it didn't seem like I was going to have much of a choice. This guy was a zombie."

"I don't care," Green snapped as she poured a packet of hot chocolate mix into a Styrofoam cup. "As far as I'm concerned, if they can commit a crime, then they can talk to me alone. If he can't answer, I just put 'Defendant refuses to answer.' End of interview. I'm not spending all day listening to family make excuses for these guys."

Ballard, although annoyed by what she considered to be Green's hard-ass exterior that thinly veiled a poor work ethic, decided to continue with her story. "Anyway, I start with all the routine stuff. The brother is doing most of the talking. And he's surprisingly open about his brother's past. He tells me that he was almost charged for

*Information and Belief*

sexually assaulting a niece a few years back, but the family agreed to have him institutionalized instead of involving the police."

"So what's your guy doing while his brother's spillin' his guts?" Moore asked.

"Nothing. He just keeps sitting there...expressionless. Anyway, I keep trying to get to my guy. I ask him a questions, he either nods or looks at his brother. It was like some twisted ventriloquist routine." Ballard sat back and took a long sip from her now lukewarm coffee. "Then, I started thinking..."

"That's never good," Bradner interrupted as he entered, having only heard the last sentence of the tale.

"In this instance, I have to agree," she continued. "Anyway, I started thinking about the training I went to last year."

"What does airborne and bloodborne pathogens have to do with this? That's the only training I got sent to last year," Crew grumbled.

"Those of us who take it upon ourselves to continue our education attend the occasional seminar...if I may be permitted to continue," she said with a sigh. "I'm referring to a training I attended regarding sex offenders. The one thing that stuck in my mind was when they were talking about collecting history on childhood abuse. They said that a lot of sex offenders have been sexually abused as children. But, if you ask them if they were abused, they'll say no. That's usually because the boundaries between normal sexual behavior and abuse can be blurred by a smooth talking perpetrator."

"What?" Moore asked with a puzzled look.

"Basically, they don't know what abuse is," she explained. "For example, you can ask them if they've been abused and they'll say no. But, later, when they're more comfortable with you, they may mention that their first sexual experience was with their baby-sitter at the age of six."

"Oh, I get ya now," Moore nodded.

"So, anyway, to cut to the chase, I look at this guy and ask, 'When was your first sexual experience?', just like they taught me." She paused and took another sip of coffee. "Then, my guy looks at his brother...his brother looks at me and says," she paused for affect..."'Do you mean with a human?'"

"Oooohhhh," the group groaned in unison.

"That's disgusting!" Crew added with a wince.

"So, what'd you do?" Natalie managed between gasps of laughter.

"I held it together pretty well. His brother went on to explain very matter-of-factly that the family had caught my guy in their barn having sex with a horse when he was about 12 years old. But the real funny thing was, this seemed to bring my guy back into the conversation. He pipes in right after, 'Yeah, but they're nothin' like the cows.'"

"Oooowwww," the group responded.

Natalie continued to laugh.

"I'm glad you find this display of bestiality so amusing," Moore chastised.

"I can't help it," she defended herself between gasps. Her ribs began to ache. "I just mentally flashed on Mister Ed saying, "Ooohhhh, Wilber." She held her sides as she continued. "Gives it a whole new meaning."

"You're a sick woman," Crew laughed.

Natalie held her hand up, index finger raised, indicating that she needed a moment as she was unable to finish her thought through her outburst. As she regained her breath, she added, "You know the medical part on the form? Where we ask about venereal disease?"

"Yes," Ballard acknowledged tentatively.

"I hope you didn't forget mad cow disease."

"Oooowwww," the group responded.

"Just to be on the safe side," Moore added, "you'd better not recommend the prison farm. The ASPCA will have your head."

"Now you've corrupted him," Ballard jokingly accused Natalie.

"That wasn't hard," Natalie responded, still laughing as she stood and began inching her way out of the room, letting the conversation continue without her.

"Animals," Crew said, shaking his head in disgust. "I've heard of puppy love, but this is ridiculous."

"Yeah, sure." Moore glanced from side to side, then rolled his eyes. "You make jokes like that and then call that guy sick."

"That means a lot coming from you," Crew laughed. "As I recall, a few weeks ago when the murderer being held at Detroit PD opted to take a dive out the 5th floor window instead of going to arraignment, and ended up a vegetable in Detroit Receiving Hospital…while people were screaming about the major design flaw in the building that would allow such a thing, you proudly proclaimed that the only design flaw at DPD was the lack of a 6th floor. Thank you Mr. Sensitive."

The voices trailed off and were replaced by the three ringing phones in the bull pen. All had a slightly different pitch or pace of alert, so she recognized the chirp of her own and snatched it up before the answering machine could take charge. "Probation, Ms. Fisher."

"Hello, is Natalie Fisher in?" a young, masculine voice inquired.

"This is Ms. Fisher."

"Oh, hi. This is Eric. How are you this morning?"

"Eric?"

"Yeah. Eric James."

"Oh, sure. Mr. James." She reached under her desk and pulled his file from the side pocket of her bag. "What can I do for you this morning?" She had fully expected this call.

"Did you get my message?"

"I haven't checked my messages this morning. What's up?"

"Well, I had your machine earlier and..."

"And now you have me," she interrupted. "What's on your mind?"

"Well, I was talkin' to my grandma yesterday and...ah...she told me about your visit."

"Yes," Natalie replied, enjoying his struggle. "She seems like a lovely woman."

"Oh yeah," he agreed readily. "But the thing is...she's kind of old fashioned. Do you know what I mean?"

"No, sir," she replied. "What exactly do you mean?"

"Well...when I said I live there...I didn't really think it was a great big deal where I live...and, anyway...I do kind of live there. I mean, I spend so much time there...you know...helping her and stuff..."

"What is your real address, sir?"

"I live with my girlfriend, Sophia, in Westland. You see, my grandma thought that it would look bad...me living with my girlfriend and all since we're not married, and..."

"Can't look any worse than lying, sir," Natalie replied flatly. She pulled a pen from her desk drawer. "What is your real address?"

"I wasn't really lying," he stammered. "I mean, I do spend a lot of time over there. It's just that…"

"What's your address, sir?" she repeated.

"We're in the apartments off Venoy Rd. You know which ones I mean?"

"The ones off the 2000 block in Westland?"

"Yeah. I think they're the only ones on Venoy. We're in number 250. It's toward the back. I always forget the exact street address since I use my grandma's but…"

"Have it for me this afternoon. I'll be by sometime between 1 and 4."

"Between 1 and 4?"

"Is there a problem with that, sir?"

"No. Not at all. I don't mind if you come. I've got nothing to hide. The thing is, I mean that's a long gap and I've got a few things to do. Could you narrow it down a bit? Give me an exact time?"

"Sir," she replied impatiently, "I did narrow it down…last time, when I went to the *last* home call." She placed a strong emphasis on the second usage of the word last. "I've got things to do, too, and one thing I don't usually have to schedule is a second home call because a person doesn't really live where they said they do. I think I'm being more than accommodating when I offer to come out again instead of telling the court you provided a fraudulent address to this department."

"No, no. That's fine. I'll be here all day."

"I'll see you between 1 and 4, sir," she confirmed curtly before hanging up.

"That must be a young one," Keller laughed, having overheard the latter part of the conversation. "I could just see you telling some F-prefix something like that.

Natalie laughed, along with Crew and Bradner, who had also rejoined them in the bull pen. The group had learned the prison code for a seasoned convict in new employee school. An inmate is given the same number every time he enters a Michigan prison. The only thing that changes is the beginning letter, or prefix. A first-time inmate starts with A, a second-timer with B, and so on.

"You have to use the intimidation factor while you have it. They learn soon enough," Natalie sighed.

"I don't think Judge Ash has even bothered to read a pre-sentence report since the Reagan administration," Crew paused briefly and added "...oh shit!"

"No need to take it so hard," Bradner countered. "Your pres are OK, but they aren't exactly what I'd call great literary classics."

Crew chose to ignore the barb. "Hey Natalie, I sure hope you don't have annual leave planned in a few weeks."

"Why is that?"

"Judge McCourt wants me and all concerned parties front and center."

"You and all concerned with what?"

"Do you remember that guy a few weeks ago? The one who came unglued when I told him I was coming to his house?"

Natalie ran a mental inventory. She'd witnessed several people who would fit the category of unglued in the past few weeks. "Oh yeah. Do you mean the guy who couldn't remember which girlfriend he lived with?"

"Yeah," he nodded.

Natalie laughed. "Mr. 'I can't be held responsible for my actions 'cause I'm on medication.'"

"That's the guy. He was on Xanax or something."

"I'm pretty sure children's Tylenol would put him over the edge. What a nut."

"Well, I ended up sending a warrant request down to court. The judge wants a hearing."

"What about Wood? Will he have to go, too?"

"I better check this out with my boss. After the run-ins Wood had with McCourt when he worked downtown, I don't think his presence will endear us to the judge." Crew scurried from the room, his eyes only leaving the paper in his right hand long enough to avoid people and furnishings.

"That just stinks," Bradner empathized. "You're going to burn a whole day just to have some judge continue this guy on probation."

"Maybe not," Natalie said with a shrug. "At least they're having a hearing. If the judge wanted to continue him, he could have done that without us." Her phone rang. "Probation, this is Ms. Fisher."

"Hi," a soft voice tentatively responded. "This is Wanda Jackson."

Natalie searched her memory. Nothing. "Good morning, Ms. Jackson," she stalled. "How can I help you?"

"I'm not sure. You left a card with my daughter. I live in the Trenton Square Apartments."

"Oh yes. Ms. Jackson, I'm sorry about that. I went to several places over the past few days." The file was still open from her conversation with Eric. She quickly scanned to the victim line. The conversation had already started on a bad note. She hated it when she didn't remember someone. She didn't want to compound the error by getting her daughter's name wrong. "I'm conducting a pre-sentence investigation on Eric James. Your daughter, Brenda, is listed as the victim of this offense. I was wondering if I could set up a time to interview you."

"Interview me for what? Hasn't he already been convicted? I thought this was done," she said irritably.

Natalie was accustomed to this response. Very few people outside of the system understand the phases of a felony criminal case. "Unfortunately, we still have the sentencing. And in order to do that, I have to complete a report about Mr. James and the circumstances of this crime and send it to the court. One of the most important circumstances is the effect this has had on your daughter and your family."

"What the hell kind of effect do you think a rape has?" she snapped defensively. "I think I'm doing the right thing. Going to work every day. That's what the welfare people say I have to do. But they don't tell you what might happen to your kids while you're out, do they? When I told those lawyers I live in Trenton Square, you'd would have thought I'd stepped in shit and tracked it into their ivory offices."

"Which lawyers, ma'am?"

"The prosecutors. First the one in Wyandotte, then the one downtown. They have me right there, but they give me some piece of paper, an impact questionnaire. It asks about our losses, like money and stuff. Then it asks what impact this had on me and my daughter. We're right there," she emphasized again. "But they want us to write it. They don't want to lower themselves to talk to us about it."

Natalie was glad she hadn't sent a questionnaire of her own, as many agents did. Some agents used it as a time-saving tool. They didn't want to bog down their schedules with in-person interviews. Some mailed it the day before they dictated the report so they could make a statement under the victim's impact heading that read, "The victim of the within offense failed to respond as of the drafting of this report." The third, and by far largest group, who relied solely on the mailing, were who Natalie called the emotional cowards. These were the agents who liked to keep their world very neat. The wide span of emotions expressed by a victim, be it anger at the perpetrator, themselves, the system, or even the questioner, complicated matters.

"I would like to meet with you and your daughter," Natalie said, "if you feel that wouldn't be too upsetting for her."

"My daughter has a dental appointment at 10:30 this morning, so I took today off. If you could come over in the late afternoon, give her a chance to let the Novocain wear off, that'd be OK."

"Would between 1:30 to 2 be all right?"

"That'd be fine."

Crew approached as Natalie hung up. "Wood is out and you're in. My boss doesn't want to take any chances on the bad blood between him and McCourt."

Bradner laughed. "Lucky you. Yet another reward for a job well done. Keeping your head and not making enemies just cost you at least half a day in court."

Natalie placed the point of her pen on the date square in question on her desktop calendar. "Did you get a time on that hearing?"

"They want us there first thing in the a.m."

Bradner laughed again. "You know what that means."

"You're enjoying this just a little too much," Natalie retorted wryly. She looked at the folder laying open before her. Then glanced back at the calendar. She felt a familiar knot in her stomach as she mentally checked off the days. *The report is due two weeks from today*, she thought. *Subtract two report days, I'm lucky to have time for a cup of coffee between interviews. Then one day in court, then Christmas Eve, Christmas Day, New Year's Eve, and New Year's Day. God, then you add the whole holiday madness. Trying to meet with anyone or get any information from the courts or PDs will be a nightmare. They'll be running skeleton crews at best. Shit!*

She turned to the residence history page of the interview booklet. Eric lived in Wyandotte with his grandmother, Westland with his girlfriend, and had a foster home placement in Woodhaven. The offense took place in Trenton. She pulled a blank notepad from her middle drawer, fingered through her rolodex, and jotted the numbers for the district courts in those cities. As was her custom, she left one half of the page empty after each number, to allow for notes.

Natalie decided to kill two birds with one stone. The cities of Trenton and Woodhaven shared the same district court. She dialed the Woodhaven District Court and was greeted by the automated system, which invited her to enter the extension of her party. Natalie punched 0 to avoid the endless loop she had found could take almost five minutes. The recorded voice instructed her: "Hold on while I try that extension." This was followed by the less cheerful voice of a living human being. "District Court."

"Hi. I'm with the State Probation Department. I need to check on a criminal disposition."

"One moment." Ten seconds of dead time was followed by two short rings. "District Court."

"Hi. This is Natalie with the State Probation Department. I'm doing a pre-sentence report on a young man out of your district and I wanted to check for misdemeanor convictions or pending cases."

"Just a minute, I have to change to that screen." A pause followed by the clicking of a fingers on a keyboard. "OK, last name?"

"James."

"Is that the last name?" the woman snapped.

"Yes, ma'am. He's got one of those interchangeable names."

"Oh yeah," she said with a laugh. "You mean Eric."

Natalie rested her elbow on her desk and rubbed her eyes. "It's just never good when you people know my guys right off the bat like that."

The woman laughed again. "It's not that bad. I'm normally the one who enters the charges, convictions, and warrants. We don't get too many CSC cases down here. Is that the one you're working on?"

"That's the one."

"You guys gonna put him away for awhile?"

"That's up to the judge. He should do some time on this. It's required by statute. But in most cases, the guy is in more trouble if you drop it to a misdemeanor and handle it at your level."

There was a pause. "What do you mean?"

"Well, if you send us a guy on...let's say a felonious assault case...that has a max of four years. Well, you and I both know when we hear the news anchor say, 'If convicted, this person faces a maximum of four years in prison,' that isn't what's going to happen. Nobody does the max. As a matter of fact, I can honestly say I've never had a guy sentenced to jail, let alone prison, for a first offense felonious assault. I mean, unless you assault Mayor Archor with a tire iron, you aren't going anywhere."

"Oh, my God. You're kidding."

"I'm not that creative. Trust me. But, on the other hand," Natalie continued, "if you guys reduce the charge to misdemeanor assault with a 90-day max, you can send him to jail."

"But why can't *you* send him to jail?" she asked incredulously.

"I suppose I should get off my soap box, but I'll finish this bitch session by complaining about the state's jail and prison space allocation. One third of the people on parole or probation are in Wayne County. We have a vast disproportion of the crime throughout the state. However, we don't get an equally disproportionate amount of the jail and prison space. So Calhoun County takes up beds in our prisons for people selling small amounts of marijuana while we can't send asaultive people for...say...domestic violence 3rd or felonious assault."

"Incredible."

Natalie sighed. "But enough about the system. Let's focus on Mr. James."

"OK. What exactly do you need?"

"Pretty much everything. I need the offense date, the original and conviction charge, the sentencing date, the docket number, and the disposition."

There was a sigh from the other side of the line. "Do you need to know what he was wearing when he was brought in, too?"

Natalie laughed. "We'll leave that for the fashion police, thanks."

There was more tapping from the keyboard. "Please tell me you don't need traffic," she pleaded. "He's got at least 20 traffic hits."

"Isn't that weird. I've noticed that most of the felons I do reports on can't drive worth a damn. Luckily, I only need those in cases that are driving-related, like negligent homicides with cars or drunk driving 3rd."

"That makes it doable. OK. Let's start here. You've got the late 95 CSC. That didn't get back to you until this year?"

"Yeah. A year from the offense to conviction isn't really that bad."

"I guess not," she agreed. "OK, we have a disorderly person, the original offense was domestic violence. He took the plea on 2/1/95. The offense date is 1/1/95."

"Happy New Year," Natalie quipped.

"That's not the way I like to celebrate."

"Yeah," Natalie agreed. "Whatever happened to chilling out in front of a football game?"

"The docket is 95-0124, C as in Cat and M as in Mouse."

"95-0124CM," Natalie repeated.

"That's it. Paid fines and costs of $250, six months non-reporting probation, and one day jail with credit for time served. Released on…wait…he was released to Plymouth PD Yeah. Looks like he had a warrant."

Natalie wrote and circled the words 'Call Plymouth.' "Anything else?"

"On 4/4/95 he was arrested for fleeing and eluding, providing false/altered identification to a police officer, and driving while license suspended. But it doesn't look like you can use that one. He pled it down to driving while license suspended and paid a $500 fine."

"Did that arrest violate his probation?" Natalie asked.

"The records show probation was administratively closed on 8/1/95. We didn't even have a probation officer on staff for four out of those six months. Besides, our judge usually only violates probation if the person commits an identical offense."

"I'm not even going to ask what the logic is behind that," Natalie said in resignation.

"Good. I'm tired of being the one to defend it."

"Anything else?"

"That's it."

"Thanks for everything. Have a good one."

"You, too."

Natalie looked up the number for the Plymouth District Court and added it to her list of calls.

"Goin' on another fishing expedition, Fisher?" Green asked sarcastically.

"What?"

"I don't know why you burn so much time callin' those district courts. If it's not on LEIN, it can't be that important."

This was a conversation Natalie was not eager to have again. "I find stuff that's not on LEIN all the time. It can make a big difference on sentencing guidelines. Besides, this is a HYTA referral. Even one misdemeanor conviction should disqualify him."

"As far as I'm concerned, if they wanted me to know, it would be on the LEIN print out. I've got 95 bodies to supervise and at least six pres a month. I'm not makin' all those calls."

"Then don't," Natalie said defensively. "If you get away with not doing it and you can live with the fact that you're being scammed by every felon that gets away with lying, why do you care what I do?"

"If you keep doin' it, then one day they're gonna get it in their heads that we should all be doin' it."

"Maybe we all *should* be doing it," Bradner added in Natalie's defense.

"If it's not in policy, I'm not doin' it." Green stalked over from her desk in the back of the bull pen to stand by the divider separating Bradner from Natalie.

"You can't reasonably expect policy to cover every possible scenario." Bradner closed his roadbook and leaned back in his chair. "Poorer cities like Inkster, River Rouge, and Ecorse don't have the manpower to enter these things into LEIN. There are days I feel lucky that the felonies are usually there."

"That's not my problem. My problem is getting these pres turned and still being able to pass the audit." Green began to walk away to insure that she had gotten the last word. "Come audit time, nobody's gonna be askin' you how many phone calls you made on your pres."

Natalie inhaled and let out a slow, long breath. She looked over to Keller, who had kept her head down and continued writing, but was exhibiting a smile that evidenced that she was listening. She heard Crew snort, attempting to suppress a laugh from behind his divider once Green was out of range.

# Chapter 31

Natalie, having finished her calls to the various courts and to juvenile records, had compiled a respectable list of charges that had been filed. However, she found that most had been pled down to far less serious convictions. This guy's lawyer knew what he was doing. He pled every violent crime to something far more benign. Whenever there were several charges and one was traffic related, he kept the traffic and took the large financial hit in exchange for pleading away the ones that could be used against him later. The cities are usually eager to accept the revenue.

She turned off her computer and put the James file in the side pouch of her bag.

"Where are you off to?" Green asked.

Natalie, although still a little steamed from their earlier run-in, kept her tone cordial. "It's going to be a long one. I've got a victim interview in Trenton and a pre home call in Westland. Then I have to shoot all the way out to the far side of Belleville to verify the residence of this guy who seems to move at least three times a year."

"I'm going to Belleville anyway. Give me the address and one of your cards to leave on the door in case he's not home."

Natalie knew this was as close to an apology as she was ever going to get from Green. "That will really take the pressure off. Thanks." Natalie wrote the address, attached a card with a paper clip, and dropped it on the yellow legal pad that lay on top of an otherwise uncluttered desk. She glanced at the pad and smiled, noting that Green had no other Belleville address on her home call agenda. *It would save her a lot of money in gas to learn to say she's sorry*, she thought.

As Natalie pulled out of the parking lot, her impulse was to drive to Trenton and conduct the victim interview first. Not because that made sense from a time management perspective, but just to leave the felon sitting on his hands for an extra hour or so. Appropriate enough, considering he had already cost her half a day attempting to verify a false address. Not to mention his attempt to hide all the misdemeanors and juvenile record. She had burned all morning calling local courts, as one kept leading to another. She winced as it struck her that this would have been the typical response from Moore or maybe Green. *God, I hope I never get that bitter or petty*, she thought as she passed the entrance to I-94, opting to take Van Born road to avoid the increased Christmas traffic by Metro Airport.

The apartments at the 2000 block of Venoy Road were a familiar stop for Natalie. Although they were not subsidized or classified as low income per se, they were located in one of the higher crime areas of the city, and lured potential tenants with a policy of charging no security deposit, asking very few questions, and a week-to-week payment option. The parking lot, to use the term loosely, was a gravel extension of the road's shoulder, deep enough to provide approximately three yards between the rear bumper of Natalie's car and southbound traffic on Venoy. A 4-foot strip of grass separated the lot from the red brick, windowless sides that faced the street. The apartments had one floor and were set in rows stretching away from the street. The front door and window of each unit in one row looked out over a sorry excuse for a courtyard, which provided an obstructed view of the front door and window in the next row. There were five apartments on each row, and the numbers went up by 10s. *That should put him in the back of the third row*, Natalie thought as she made her way down the stone path.

She noted the building number, 2030, as she turned the corner. She heard country western music from behind the first door. The second and third were silent. In the next unit a baby was crying, while a pathetic young voice was pleading, "Will you please just shut up!"

Natalie stood on the step of apartment 250. She heard movement. Quiet mumbles and a chair scraping along a floor. She knocked. She heard a few more quick whispers, an inner door closed. She caught movement out of the corner of her eye. The drapes separated slightly, then fell back into place.

The door opened. Eric James smiled broadly. "Miss Fisher, come on in." He stood to one side and motioned with his hand.

Natalie returned his smile and sidestepped past him, never completely turning her back on her host and maintaining her position as closest to the door handle.

"Sorry about the mix-up." He moved to the center of the room. "But here we are now. This is it," he added nervously.

"Mix-up?" Natalie asked.

"Yeah. The address thing. I'm sorry if it wasted any of your time. But, I guess you had to talk to my grandma anyway. So, no real harm done, huh?"

"Ah, I see," Natalie said aloud while thinking, *Bold faced lie is more what I'd call it.* She wasn't going to confront him, but she wasn't going to feed his minimization tactics either. "Who else is here?"

"What do you mean?"

"I mean who else is here?" she repeated.

"I live here with my girlfriend. You saw her in the lobby when I was at your office, remember? But she's not here now."

"I thought I heard you talking to someone." Natalie looked toward the door on the other side of the room. "I thought I heard that door close."

"Well, yeah, you did. I mean she's home, in the other room. But she's not in here with us now. She's asleep. Or trying to sleep, I should say. She hasn't been feeling good."

"I see," she said with a nod. The furnishings in the small living room and attached kitchen were worn, but clean. She could see no dishes in the sink from her vantage point, and the rug appeared to have been recently vacuumed. "The flu? A lot of that going around lately."

"Yeah, she's been throwin' up all night. Would you like to sit down?" he offered as he walked to the couch.

Natalie chose the wooden chair closest to the door. Her experience as a child welfare worker contributed to this selection. She was far less likely to leave with more than she arrived with…be it lice, cockroaches, or the like. Soft, cushy furniture were breeding grounds for those. On one occasion, she had sat in an unknown slimy substance that necessitated a midday trip home and a large tip to a surly dry cleaner.

"Just a couple of things I'd like to clarify, if we might." She opened the file and leafed through some notes. "Besides your address, are there any other things that you'd like to clear up? Any other possible…oversights on your part?"

He sat quietly for a moment, leaning forward, his elbows on his knees, resting his chin in one open hand. He stared at the wall, then ran his hands through his hair and let out a long breath. "Look, I know it doesn't look good. But you've gotta believe me. I'm not, like, a bad guy. I'm not some maniac that jumps out of the bushes at women in the middle of the night. I'm not out in school yards offering candy to little kids." His eyes welled up and he quickly looked away. "I was just...well, I don't know if you know what this means or not. It might be a guy thing." He regained his composer and was now looking directly at Natalie. "I was what they call a player. I said or did whatever I had to. Whatever a girl wanted to hear. I'm not proud of that now. Things have changed. I just found out that I'm goin' to be a dad. I don't want my son to have to say that his dad was in jail." He paused. "You can't send me to jail," he said almost inaudibly.

"Please understand," Natalie said solemnly, "I don't send anyone to jail or prison. Only a judge can make that decision. Did your lawyer review the guidelines with you?"

"He said that most of it depends on your report."

Natalie hesitated. Her first inclination was to remind him that the offense carried a 1-year minimum. *God, I hate talking to people in the field*, she thought. "You should probably review that with you lawyer. Michigan does have sentencing guidelines and statutory minimums. Believe me, judges who spent four years in college, three in law school, and endless hours clerking for others...not to mention all the money it takes to get elected...they're not sitting on their hands waiting for some community college probation officer to tell them what to do. I mean, I'm not exactly E.F. Hutton."

"Who?"

"You know, E.F. Hutton, like on the commercials. Never mind. It's not that important. Anyway, what I'm trying to say is that the judge will make up his own mind. The guidelines are based in law. Your lawyer should be able to give you a good idea of what you're looking at...as long as you told him the truth about your prior record, that is."

"What do you mean, if I told him about my record? He looked at my record. So did you."

"Mr. James, I don't want to go into all of that now."

"Are you sayin' there's somethin' else? I saw my record in court," he said defensively.

151

"I don't have all of my notes with me, sir. If you want to call me at the office tomorrow, that would be fine. I'd be happy to review what I have if you don't think it's accurate." She rose and stepped quickly to the door.

He followed close behind. "I'm not saying I don't think you're accurate. But, I mean...we had a printout at court."

"Maybe you're right," Natalie said soothingly as she left. "I wouldn't want to guess without my notes and get you all upset over nothing."

"OK, well, I'll do that. I'll call you tomorrow. But do you know what you're gonna recommend?"

"Not yet, sir. I still have calls to make." Natalie gave a friendly wave. "I'll talk to you soon." She felt his eyes on her back and was relieved when she heard him step back into the apartment and close the door.

She had already fished the last time sheet out of the red folder, which had been obscured by the client report forms and pre-sentence dictation guide, when she realized she had left her pen on the dining room table.

"Damn!" She considered leaving it. If it were just another cheap ball point, one of the three left yearly in her mailbox by the state's pen fairy, she would have. Although not a Mont Blonc, it was a nice thick, sturdy pen and had been a gift from Gwen on her last birthday.

She walked back up the row of doors. *I hate this. I come off looking like someone who watched too many Detective Columbo reruns.* "Just one more thing, sir..." she could hear the short fellow in the wrinkled raincoat say while making exaggerated gestures, cigar in hand.

She practiced her apology for disturbing him again in her head as she knocked. The door opened. As Natalie opened her mouth to begin, she caught the first word in her throat before it could betray her. "Mr. James," she had meant to say. But it was not Mr. James. Natalie recognized the young woman as the one in the lobby. The one that had looked so lost when she had been left to fend for herself as Natalie had foiled her boyfriend's plan to use her as a symbol of his age-appropriate sexual attraction. The girl had a bruise the shape of a half moon, if the moon were to fall over, leaving the open side

*Information and Belief*

up, under her left eye. She had a scrape about the size of a half dollar on the right side of her forehead.

"Ma...ah...Miss. I hate to trouble you, but I think I..."

James appeared in the doorway, towering over the frail young girl. He smiled, put one arm gently around her back, gripping her shoulder tightly and pulling her to him. He presented the pen with his free hand. "Looking for this?"

Natalie took the pen and, turning her attention back to the young woman, stated apologetically, "I'm sorry. I know we met before, but I've forgotten you name."

"Sophia," she responded softly.

"That's right. Are you feeling better?"

Sophia glanced uneasily at her boyfriend. "I'm much better, thanks." Sensing that Natalie was waiting for an explanation, she quickly added, "I'd be a lot better if I'd quit walking into doors."

Eric laughed. It was a tight, tense sound. "It wasn't all your fault, baby. If I hadn't been coming in so quickly." He continued with a sheepish smile. "I was comin' in and I was real excited about that raise I got at work...oh, yeah...did you talk to my boss yet?"

"Not yet," Natalie said. "You were saying...about coming in."

"Yeah. Here I was, real excited and all and I just came stormin' in."

"And there I was...like a dope...just standing by the front door, and wham," the girl concluded, putting her hand to the darkened eye.

Natalie, while standing in the doorway, opted not to ask about the scrape on the other side of her face. "Isn't that always the way," she said. She held up the pen. "Thanks. I have several other stops. I really have to go."

"No problem," Eric assured her. "If you'd left it, I would have run it up to you. No problem."

"Thanks again," she said, taking a few steps backward before turning toward the lot.

## Chapter 32

Natalie was caught off guard at a door for the second time in one day. *I need to stop assuming who'll be on the other side of the door*, she thought.

Wanda Jackson just wasn't what she'd expected. The tired, pessimistic voice should have belonged to…well…she wasn't quite sure what. But not to this woman. Tall, slim, with sharp features. Natalie's first impression of the woman's wardrobe instantly made her feel underdressed. Natalie reserved her dry-cleanable suits for those rare court appearances. As she entered the apartment, she was struck by a smell that she could only describe as fresh. Not a perfumed, commercial fresh like some housewife blasting the atmosphere with a pine or lemon scent. Just clean. And the best kind of clean. Clean without being hospital-like and sterile. It was homey. A few things out of place, what she would call lived in, but with an underlying sense of order. *Oh, God. It's happened. You've become the kind of person who expects to walk in and find empty beer cans and dishes stacked by the sink.* On the other hand, she thought, continuing the internal dialog as she was ushered to a seat at the kitchen table, *the dishes and occasional beer can sound more like my house on a bad day. Sometimes on a good day.*

"Would you like a glass of water?" Ms. Jackson opened the refrigerator. "We have some Pepsi I think."

"No. I'm fine, thanks." She took out a pen and flipped past the page with her never-ending to-do lists and scribbled afterthoughts. She had never found a good way to start an interview with a victim. Asking what happened can open wounds. On the other hand, if you don't ask, and they want to talk about it, you look like a coward who doesn't have the guts to hear their pain. Or worse, a bureaucrat who doesn't care. If you start by asking about financial losses, you likely get the defensive response, "This is not about money." She gave God one last moment to provide her with an epiphany. When none came, she launched in.

"Did you want to start this interview with your daughter, or are there any matters you'd like to discuss before you call her?"

"I'll get her in a minute," Ms. Jackson responded as she took the seat across from Natalie. "I just wanted to say...well...if I came off a little bitchy on the phone, I'm sorry." She leaned back and took an ashtray off the counter. Free of ashes, it contained a partial pack of Winston's and a butane lighter. She snapped her wrist, releasing and reestablishing her grip to eject a single cigarette. She put the end to her lips, never looking at the pack, as though the possibility of error, a smoke falling to the floor, two white sticks instead of one, was inconceivable.

"This has been going on for months," she continued. "Everyone asks the same questions. Why do you leave your daughter home alone? Why did she let him in?" She drew the smoke in deeply. The tiny snapping sound of the dried tobacco seemed unusually loud, as it had no competition.

Natalie wondered what the victim was doing. With no television or radio on, Natalie would work under the assumption that the girl was sitting quietly, listening from the next room. "I won't be asking any questions like that today ma'am," she said, projecting a smile that she hoped would lighten the mood. "When people come to me, they've already been convicted, or pled guilty. I personally don't think that a person who is completely innocent of wrongdoing would plead guilty to a crime that would require him to serve time and be registered for life as a sex offender."

"But he's been around, telling all his buddies that he's got this big-time lawyer and he's not going to jail over some slut. Some slut!" she repeated, with more emphasis, but in a hushed tone. "Do you have any idea what it's like to have your neighbors repeat something like that to you about your own daughter?"

"No, I don't. But that's really why I'm here. I want to make your experience a part of the record. It's not my intent to have your daughter go through the pain of reliving what happened. Although I will add that a lot of children seem to benefit from telling their story. And I'll be happy to listen for as long as she wants to talk."

"I don't see no benefit. She's had everything that she did that day picked apart by police and prosecutors and..."

"I see what you're saying," Natalie interrupted. "What I mean is that they benefit from telling their story to someone who believes them. And I'll tell you, I've read the police reports and I've interviewed Mr. James. I have no doubt in my mind that your daughter is telling the truth. And, I'd like to add, I talked briefly to the detective on this case. I didn't get the impression that he doubted your daughter."

Wanda sighed as she exhaled the last drag from her cigarette and smashed it out in the ashtray. "People keep telling me that they're just doing their job. But they don't seem to care what their job does to us."

"This is your chance to say that to the court, Ms. Jackson." Natalie clicked her pen and began taking notes. "You've already told me that this has caused you a great deal of pain because you feel that the system has attempted to blame you and your daughter. What other effects have this incident had on your life?"

"It's caused me problems on my job. I've had to miss days for court to take my daughter down to the police for interviews. She missed school. Had to do a rape kit even though they knew they wouldn't find anything. It was too late by the time she told me. She'd already taken a shower. They knew damn well that he'd say she wanted to have sex with him anyway."

"Where are you working?"

"I'm a receptionist at a dental office. It's part time. Five hours a day. No weekends. I thought it would be the perfect job. I'd be home when my daughter got home and…well…" Her voice drifted off.

"Were the medical expenses covered by insurance? And how many days work did you miss?"

"Three. It doesn't sound like much, but our budget is tight. Not to mention how ticked off the office manager was."

"How much are you earning per hour?"

"Why would you need to know that for your report?"

"I know it's a very personal question. But one of the things I can recommend is that the defendant reimburse you for your losses. If I can show the court documentation of missed days, most judges will order the defendant to pay. We can also request that he be required to pay for any counseling…"

"No way," she said angrily. "I don't want you putting anything in there about him giving us any money."

*Information and Belief*

"It sounds like you have a real problem with this whole money issue." Natalie spoke in a soft tone, hoping to de-escalate the situation. "I can assure you that this is a very common request made in most instances where there is a victim."

"You just don't get it."

"You're right, I don't. I never will if you don't tell me." Natalie's tone was a little sharper, a bit more defensive than she'd wanted it. She scrambled to recover. "What I mean is, I want to fairly represent your feelings in this report. I need you to help me understand them so I can put them into words."

"What you don't understand is that I live here. If someone on the other side of the street went to court and asked for money, they'd call it justice. If I do that, then their eyebrows go up. They think, 'Oh, I see, this whole thing was really just about money.' Well, I'm telling you this, we don't need that man's money. This isn't about money. We want him in jail so I won't have to worry when I let my daughter out of the house."

Natalie scribbled notes. "That's clear enough. Is there anything you'd like to add?"

"Just that I want him to stay the hell away from here. At night sometimes he comes driving past here and blares the radio when he gets to our part of the parking lot. I've looked out the window and seen him there, just glaring at me. By the time the police get here, he's gone. My daughter doesn't sleep the night through anymore"

"I'll be sure to bring it to the judge's attention. When someone is put on probation or parole, they can have the judge order that he have no contact with you or your family. He might even ban him from your complex so he can't play these kind of games. Is there anything else?"

"You know he's done this before, right? There are two other girls who live in this same complex. From what I hear, he didn't force them like he did Brenda, but they were so young, they really didn't know what he was doing."

"I did hear that other allegations were made in the past, but it sounds like they didn't follow through. Do you have any idea why that is?"

She scoffed and shook her head in disbelief. "Have you been listening to a word I'm saying? If I'd have known then what I know

now, I'm not sure we would have gone to the police." She stood up and walked through the living room. "I'll get my daughter."

She returned with the slightly built, dark-haired girl who had greeted Natalie at the door on her first visit. "This is my daughter, Brenda." She turned to face the girl. "Brenda, this woman just wants to ask you a few things about the whole thing with Eric. I'll leave you two to talk." She turned back toward Natalie. "How long will you be?"

"I'll spend as much time as Brenda is comfortable with," Natalie replied, hoping to set the girl at ease. "Brenda, I know you've had to talk to a lot of people about a lot of personal things. I'm really not here to make you do that again."

"What is it you want to know?" she asked plaintively. "First I had to talk to a policeman in a uniform, then a detective. Then I had to talk to the prosecutor at the Woodhaven court. Then I had to testify in front of the judge. I thought that was all there would be. But then they said we'd have to go to the court downtown. It started all over again. I had to talk to a different prosecutor. He said I was going to have to tell the story to another judge and a jury unless we let him take a plea."

"I know it's been difficult. That's really why I'm here. I want to know how you feel about everything that's happened. I just need to tell the judge how you're doing now."

"I'm OK," she said quietly.

*This is going to be like pulling teeth*, Natalie thought. She decided to start with the basics that she heard from most victims with the hope that she could get her talking. "Have you had any problems in school? Trouble sleeping?"

"I missed a lot of school. First to talk to the police, then to go to court. Then kids in school started to find out. His big mouth brother told everyone that I lied on his brother and now he's in trouble."

"How long have you known his brother?"

"He was in my class this year. I'd seen him around school the year before, but I hadn't talked to him. After this happened and he started giving me trouble, my mom got me moved to another class."

"That must have been hard."

"Well, it just didn't seem fair to me. How come I had to change classes?"

*Information and Belief*

"You're right. It's not fair."

"It's just like this whole thing they want to give him. After he finishes probation, he won't have any record. He gets to just forget about it. How come I don't get to just forget about it?"

"His attorney has requested HYTA. But that doesn't mean he'll get it. First, we..."

"Oh, he'll get it all right. He's got his mom and step-dad paying for it. If he doesn't get it, then he'll just take back his plea and I'll have to go to court. He said that since we'd already...well, you know we'd done it before," she said softly, her eyes cast toward the floor. "He said it's not rape if we'd already done it before."

"That's just not true Brenda. A person always has the right to..."

"Sure!" she continued in a mocking tone. "It's your body. You always have the right to say no. That's what people like you and the counselors at the crisis center say. But that's not how people, you know, people who count like judges and lawyers feel. If they felt that way, he'd be going to prison and he'd have a record."

"He will do some time for this. A conviction for CSC 3rd carries a mandatory prison sentence in the state of Michigan. Guidelines for this incident should be a little higher than that."

"That's not what his brother says. His lawyer says he won't even have to lose his job."

"Lawyers say a lot of things. Sometimes their clients hear what they want to hear. By the time that message gets to their family and friends, the real message is very different."

"It doesn't matter. It's over." The pitch and volume of her voice escalated. "I'm just not going to think about it anymore. If he doesn't have to, then I don't have to."

Wanda Jackson returned with a look of apprehension. "What's going on here?" she asked, glancing from one face to another.

"I'm not doing this anymore," the girl said. "I don't care what happens to him." She walked past her mother, slamming the door.

There was an uncomfortable silence. Natalie broke it. "I'm sorry." She put her notes into her folder. "I'm usually much better at this. I've obviously upset her. I guess I should of..."

"It wouldn't have mattered. That's how she's been since it happened. One minute she's fine, then the next she's storming off somewhere." She walked Natalie to the door.

"She said something about some counselors. Is she still going?"

"She went a few times. She doesn't like it. Says they do nothing but talk."

"Well, when the time seems right, you might want to reintroduce the idea. It's no miracle cure, but most people I've talked to years after something like this say it helps."

"Yeah, thanks for your help. We'll think about that." Her tone reminded Natalie of the one she used when she assured the Jehovah's Witnesses that she'd read their literature as soon as she got a free moment.

# Chapter 33

Natalie put her bag beside the door and fumbled for the light. She felt like a vampire at this time of year. It was dark when she left the house in the morning and was dusk by the time she got home. As draining as it could be, she was grateful for the field work that allowed her to catch a peek at the sun. Gwen hadn't made it home before 8:30 all week. The layoff crisis had passed with a new contract that was signed with General Motors.

The cat scurried to the bowl. Although it was half full, the animal was never at peace either in the morning or when Natalie returned from work, until she added at least a few kernels.

She pushed the play button on the answering machine before opening the freezer door to review the frozen dinner possibilities. Two hang-ups were followed by the whining voice of Gwen's mother. "Gweeeeen," she began, "your father and I..." At this point, her father's traditional "Hello," then a pause, as though his next thought took some mental formation, "It's your dad here."

"She knows that, Paul," her mother chastised. "Gwen, your father and I were just wondering if, at some point, we could get together with you and your brother and..."

*God bless my parents*, Natalie thought as she listened to the remains of the rambling message, interrupted only by the couple's parenthetical squabbles.

Beep. "It's me." Gwen's recorded voice never did justice to the soothing tone Natalie had grown to love. "I'll be late. Roger has me working with him all week on another project and..."

"Awwww," Natalie groaned. She knew on one level that success in the private sector required more time and effort. Her father was evidence of that. Memories of contact with him other than vacations were limited. He considered his role to be that of provider. He did that well. He also died at 55. No coincidence in Natalie's mind.

Beep. "This message is for Natalie," a cheerful voice greeted. "This is Kim from Dr. Young's office. It's time for your six month checkup. Please call between the hours of..."

*That'll be the day.* Natalie, having a life-long fear of any dental care more intrusive than daily brushing, only went to the dentist when the pain of not going surpassed her personal tolerance level.

Beep. "Hi, Gwen. It's Dave. Just wanted to let you know that the meeting has been pushed up from 9 to 8:30. We got bumped from the conference room since quality is holding it's training there. We'll use Roger's office since he's on vacation. Be sure to bring your department's budget proposal and..."

*Work late, start early,* Natalie grumbled.

"This is Jerry King, the Gutter Doctor. We'll be in your neighborhood giving estimates on repairs and new installations. There is no obligation..."

"Wait a minute," Natalie said aloud as she rewound the machine.

"...is holding it's training there. We'll use Roger's office since he's on vacation."

Natalie rewound further.

"I'll be late. Roger has me working with him all week..."

Natalie's stomach dropped. *There must be another explanation. Just think. She could have misspoken. She might have meant that she was working for Roger, not with him. Or maybe Dave meant another Roger.*

Natalie dialed Gwen's number. It went to voice mail after four rings. She hung up, and after finding Gwen's work directory in the desk, dialed Roger's number. *This is stupid. What am I going to say if he answers?*

"Hello," a recorded voice answered. "You have reached the office of Roger Martin. I will be out of the office for the remainder of the month. Please contact Jack Billings in the event that your business is of an urgent nature. Thank you." A short tone followed as Natalie hung up.

"Stop it," she said aloud to herself. "You'll just ask her when she gets home. I'll wait up, talk about my day, and wait to hear if maybe there's some logical explanation."

She zapped a TV dinner in the microwave and turned on the set. She started with Jeopardy and fell asleep on the couch somewhere after Leno's monologue.

"Wake up babe," Gwen whispered, gently rubbing her back. "You're going to be feel every bump on this old couch in the morning if you don't come to bed."

"What time is it?"

"It's late," were the last words she remembered before her alarm the next morning.

## Chapter 34

Natalie entered the back door of the probation office. Gwen had left by the time Natalie awoke. *Maybe just as well,* she thought. *What was I going to say?* She had no frame of reference. She'd had her share of relationship problems, but a cheating partner had never been one of them. Money, friends, family, career. These were areas she could relate to.

"You're not my mama!" a voice bellowed from Matthews' office. "Not you and not the court can tell me I can't drink! It's legal. It's legal in this country to drink."

"I understand that," Matthews responded calmly. "But we both know that bad things tend to happen when you drink. You acknowledged that in court and agreed with the judge's decision…"

"That's bullshit! My lawyer told me that this judge is soft on anybody who says they drink and need help. He said as long as I didn't get into any more trouble while I was drinking, it wouldn't be any big deal."

"Then this is a problem of your own creation. There are no refunds when you sell your soul to the devil."

"What?"

"You signed the probation order."

*Really, how do you nicely ask someone if they lied to you?* Natalie wondered as she passed the quiet offices of agents Jefferson, Dowd, and Keller.

"You can't be serious," Moore said in a bitter tone, seemingly to the paper he was holding.

Natalie's heart dropped as she made eye contact with him and realized that she wasn't going to get away without an early morning whine-fest. "I told you to never start your day with the memos," she said. "Memos should only be removed from your mailbox or reviewed between the hours of 10 a.m. and 3:30 p.m."

"They screw with our minds enough. Screwing with our money is too much."

Natalie took the paper from his hands. "They can't do that. We have a union." She noted the date of the policy directive. "There can't be anything new here. This hasn't been updated in years."

*Information and Belief*

He came around the desk, taking the pages and shuffling to the attached policy directive.

"Uh oh," she said. "Not the dreaded director's memorandum."

"Yep. The department's way of changing the rules in the middle of the game."

Natalie flipped the pages, trying to follow the referenced sections for the new interpretation. "I get it...no wait..." She flipped back. "No. That can't be...wait. Let me start over."

"Let me save you the trouble. I heard rumblings of this from the supervisor's office, but I never thought the union would let them get away with it."

"Please," Natalie chastised. "We're UAW. You'd have to make three calls before you convinced our local representative that you don't build cars." She flipped through the pages again. "I've got stuff to do. Can I get the *Reader's Digest* version?"

"We've always gotten paid premium mileage, 30 cents a mile."

"Right."

"Well, now they're saying that we can only do that if a state car isn't available."

"That hasn't changed. It's always said that. We've never had a state car for this office."

"That's the new catch. Now we do."

"That's great. The agents who lease will be thrilled."

"I doubt that. The car will be located in a lot at the State Building."

"That's a 25-mile round trip..."

"With our probationers on the other side of the county," Moore finished.

"So, we're cut back to 25 cents a mile?"

"That's right."

Natalie tossed the memo on her desk, grabbed her coffee cup and repeated her mantra, "Never start with the memos, never start with the memos," as she walked to the break room.

"What?" Joan asked, looking up from her cup.

"Nothing I want to dwell on this early. How's Elds? Has she heard anything?" Natalie asked.

"Nothing. They haven't even set a hearing date."

"She's bound to win. Nobody stays fired from the state. We have people who only show up for work about three times a year, and *they* keep their jobs."

"That's easy to say. She'll probably get her job back. She might get back pay. But her reputation is shot, and she has to find a way to pay her bills during the process."

Natalie took the pot from the burner and filled both cups.

"What really gets me," Joan continued, "is that every felon who walks in here is treated better. I've had guys sentenced to probation on their 9th felony. An agent with an outstanding record will have to sell her house to get by while Mr. Nine gets a court-appointed attorney."

"Is she really losing her house?"

"She's got nothing coming in. I don't see what else…"

"Aw, I can't believe we're out of decaf," Moore yelled as he picked up the empty pot.

"Will the madness never end?" Natalie mocked as she poured herself a cup of coffee.

Moore held out his cup.

"I don't know. I really don't think caffeinated is the way for you to go," Natalie laughed, pulling the pot away.

"Don't make me use my weapon, Fisher. I'm a man on the edge."

Natalie filled his cup. "That's right. Nothing like a little shot of caffeine to take care of that."

"Fisher, you got any community service sites that are taking probationers right now?" Green asked.

"A few, but it really depends on the offense. What'd your guy do?"

"Not a guy," she responded. "You'll like this one. This woman takes her father out of the nursin' home." She filled her cup with water and put it in the microwave. "Tells them she can take care of old dad just fine and she don't know what they're spendin' his whole SSI check on." Interrupted by the beep of the microwave timer, she removed her cup, opened her tea bag, and slowly lowered it into the steaming water. "So she and her family, who in my eyes just wanted that ol' man's check, they're livin' in one of those run-down, rent-by-the-week hotel rooms with a kitchenette on Michigan Ave."

"Ugh," Moore interjected. "I've had a bunch of guys in those. They're just disgusting."

"The Hilton it's not." She raised and lowered the bag by its string as she continued. "Bein' the good daughter that she is," she said sarcastically, "they give pops his own room."

"Sweet location," Moore laughed. "Puts the old man just a two-minute push in his chair from some of the finest adult movies Inkster has to offer."

"You know what they say in the real estate game," Natalie added. "Location, location, location."

"So, anyway," Green continued, "one day the 12-year-old decides to look in on ol' gramps. Mom and dad had gone and the key to his room was on the dresser." She chuckled. "Ironically, they'd gone out to eat. Anyway, this poor kid goes in and finds what's left of gramps."

"What's left?" Moore asked hesitantly.

"The old guy was dead. Stinking up the place in the middle of June. No windows open. The police report says the exam showed that he hadn't been fed in at least five days. None of his meds were in his system. Said his blood had completely dried up. Flys, maggots, the whole nine yards."

"Yuck! Glad I'm not a big breakfast eater," Moore responded with disgust.

"I guess you won't be surprised to learn that she casually acknowledged that she was sexually abused by her father when she was 12."

"Guess she's over it now," Moore laughed.

"She claims that had nothing to do with it. She just kind of calmly said that they forgot he was there."

Natalie burst into laughter. "I...I guess..." She stopped and caught her breath. "I guess Meals on Wheels is definitely out as her community service placement."

Green huffed in exasperation as Natalie and Moore laughed. "You people are sick. When you're over it, Fisher, come by with your rolodex."

Natalie couldn't stop. She shouted to Green as she left, "It'll be the first time in organizational history that they ran in the black. I can hear 'um now. 'Why do we have so much damn food?'"

"Wait a minute," Moore said angrily when she was out of voice range. "Can you imagine what would happen if you or I said 'You people,' to her, being black? She'd have us under investigation."

"Oh, man," Natalie mooned. "Let's not go there this morning."

"But it's exactly the same thing," he protested.

"It's not the same thing," Natalie countered as she refilled her cup. "Intent is everything. She wasn't condemning our race. It's you and I she thinks are sick."

"Thanks," he sulked. "I feel much better now."

Natalie took her coffee back to her desk. The bull pen was in full swing.

Crew was midway through his pre-sentence intro spiel. "It's important that you be as open and honest as possible because I have to verify everything you tell me here today."

Keller was prepped for report day. Drug test chain of custody forms neatly stacked on the right front portion of her desk, bottles lined against the side that meets the wall.

Wood was interviewing a dirty, unshaven man with greasy hair. Natalie knew the man must smell like last week's road kill, because Wood had his "funk fan" on high, blowing toward Keller, who patiently accepted the situation.

Natalie took her rolodex, holding her breath as she passed Wood's desk. At Green's desk she said, "For community service, I guess daddy's little girl can't do too much harm folding clothes at the Salvation Army used store."

"Thanks," Green said curtly. She jotted the numbers Natalie gave her on a notepad.

Natalie returned to her desk. She wanted to call Gwen, but there was no way she'd get a moment alone, outside of a fortuitous bomb scare. She'd wait until she could get out and use her car phone.

"Look, man," Crew's man protested. "The police, they got it all wrong."

"There's not much to get wrong," Crew answered sternly. He continued to write while he spoke. "The police responded to a silent alarm and found you inside the Little Caesar's Pizza Parlor trying to break into the coin box of their pay phone."

"Naw man, I was…"

*Information and Belief*

"It really doesn't matter. Your day in court is over. We're not here to decide if you're guilty."

"But listen! It's like this. I made myself some homemade wine and me, not bein' used to drinkin', I got real drunk real fast."

Crew put his pen on the desk, deciding not to fight the inevitable explanation.

"So, bein' drunk, me and the ol' lady, we gets into a fight. So I decides, I better go for a walk befo' this gets outa hand. So, I'm goin' fo' my walk. But instead a gettin' coolt off, I just keeps gettin' madder and madder. I don't want to go home with all these angry feelings. So, I picks up dis brick and I throws it at the nearest thing, a winda'. But, instead of it breakin', it bounces off and hits me in the head. Well, I falls into the winda' and I fall right into the building. I was tryin' to call fo' help when the police, they come runnin' in and hauls me off to jail. Shit! They wouldn't listen to nothin'."

Crew looked at the police report. "How did the cash register get broken and the money get into your pocket?"

"Shit man! Dat's just the po po tryin' to make thereselves look big. Dat money was from my job. Da people what owns dat pizza place, day jus' wanna screw dare insurance company. Dey don't care what happens to me."

"Po po?" Crew asked.

"Po po," he reiterated, emphasizing the o sound. "Da Pooolice."

"That's a new one," Crew replied. He jotted the term on the pad that he kept by his phone, just to the left of his message pad. The words 'Street Slang' appeared at the top. Crew, a life-long suburbanite, always felt he was playing catch-up with the ever-changing language of the street.

Natalie pulled the James file from the rack and ran down the checklist attached to the cover. Drug Test = negative. Co-defendants = none. Juvenile Court File = 93-730983. Reviewed = Local PDs, Trenton, Woodhaven, Lincoln Park. LEIN = criminal record and traffic. Victim Interview = complete. Other = Interview with private therapist. Family Interview = Grandmother. Sentencing Guidelines = 18 to 32 months.

*Ready to dictate*, she thought. She put a tape in the Dictaphone. "Testing, one, two, three. Testing." She spoke softly, being as considerate as possible in such close quarters. The tape squealed as it rewound. "Testing, one, two, three. Testing." She winced, hating the sound of her own voice on tape. She took a breath and tried to clear her mind. She pushed the red button.

"Evaluation and Plan. Before the court is a 20-year-old single male. He currently resides with his girlfriend, who is expecting their first child, in the city of Westland. He is a high school graduate and is employed as an assembler in an auto-parts factory.

"The defendant is before the court for sentencing on three counts of CSC 3rd. The conviction and referral slip reflects that this case is under consideration for HYTA status. The defendant's prior criminal record consists of misdemeanor convictions for trespassing, fleeing and eluding the police, disorderly person, and providing false ID to police. Additionally, he has one juvenile adjudication for assault and battery.

"The victim of the within offense, 12-year-old Brenda Jackson, reports that she has missed school as a result of harassment on the part of persons representing the defendant. Her mother reports that the defendant has driven by the home, yelling profanities, and once confronted her, standing and staring in the front window of her home. She is requesting that the court order the defendant to have no contact with her or her family. It is further recommended by this writer that the defendant be prohibited from making any contact with the victim or her family via a third party. The family is not requesting restitution.

"The defendant's strengths include his attainment of a high school diploma, active participation in counseling, and current employment.

"Negatively, the defendant has expressed no remorse regarding his involvement in the within offense. When interviewed, the defendant told this writer, 'You don't understand, girls like that (the defendant was referring to those living in subsidized housing) expect to be treated a certain way.' Additionally, the defendant has a prior criminal record which excludes him from HYTA consideration. Finally, it should be noted that the defendant made numerous misrepresentations regarding his criminal past and living situation to this writer during the course of the pre-sentence investigation.

"Sentencing guidelines…"

*Information and Belief*

Natalie paused as she shuffled through the file. She switched the Dictaphone off. *Shit, I forgot to do the guidelines. Don't panic. These'll just take a second.*

"PRVs. Prior record variables," she mumbled as she pulled a sentencing information report from her drawer.

She read aloud. "Prior high severity felony convictions = 0. Prior low severity = 0. Juvenile high severity = 0. Low severity = 0. Misdemeanor convictions, let's see, the false ID, fleeing and eluding, and trespassing don't score. Only crimes in the groups of burglary, CSC, drug, fraud, larceny, property destruction, robbery or weapons count. The disorderly, well, pled down from DV. I'll score it. Give his lawyer something to argue about. Then there's the juvenile A & B. Two priors counts = 5 points. Then, prior relationship to the criminal justice system equals = 15 points, for being on probation for disorderly when he picked up this case. Subsequent or concurrent felony conviction = 20 points for the other two counts. Total, 40."

Natalie checked the grid. Prior record variables was the 3rd level, C, on the grid.

She moved to the offense variables. She pulled the police report from the file to reference. OV1, Aggravated use of a weapon. She didn't need the report for this. No weapon = 0. OV2, Physical attack and/or injury. Natalie was tempted to score the 50 points for excessive brutality. She felt all rapes were brutal. But she knew that, like most big cities, Wayne County's definition of brutal required stitches in the double digits. She scored 25 for bodily injury based on the fingernails broken below the quick, and the fact that the girl had been subjected to a rape kit. Keep that high paid lawyer busy. OV5, Victim was carried away or held captive. She wasn't taken anywhere. Although he prevented her from leaving when he committed the offense, she wasn't held beyond the point necessary to commit the offense. Apparently, the legislature thinks this is a mitigating factor. Zero points. OV6, Multiple victims = 0 points for only one victim. OV7, Offender exploitation of Victim Vulnerability.

The highest points were reserved for exploitation due to authority, disability, youth, or agedness. Although the victim was young, Natalie knew that this was reserved for tricking or coercing a child. She'd seen many adult women fall for the charm con this guy used to get in the door. She scored 5 points for his exploitation, based on size and strength difference. OV9, Offender's role. A one-offender crime is 0 points. OV12, Criminal Sexual Penetrations. Natalie reviewed the instructions. The penetrations that make up the count, that is to say, the thing that separates what most people call rape from molestation, can only be scored if there are more penetrations than counts. Since they charged him on all three penetrations, he gets no points here. He already got his points for that under the prior record variables, for being convicted on more than one count. Zero points here. OV13, Psychological Injury to Victim. This is a given in most courtrooms. Five points for need for counseling to the victim. OV25, Contemporaneous Criminal acts. This is only scored if counts are dropped, or in some cases, if it is ongoing, like a child who claims that dad molested her every night for a year. He won't be convicted on all of them, but he's held accountable, depending on the judge, on this variable. Nothing for Mr. James here. Zero points.

She totaled the count: 35. It fell between 25 and 49. This put him in the Roman Numeral III section. Now it was just like a football pool, or a map. Follow the III line across to the C line, which came down from the top. The points met at 48 to 120 months.

She cleared her throat and returned to her dictation.

"Sentencing guidelines reflect a range of 48 to 120 months. Incarceration is mandated by statue. Due to the nature of the offense, the defendant does not qualify for alternative programming."

A voice interrupted Natalie. "I don't need this number." She looked up in time to see a piece of white notepaper flutter toward Keller's face.

"Sir," Keller said in a curt tone.

"I don't need…"

"Sir," Keller repeated. "Do not interrupt me."

*Not the best de-escalation technique*, Natalie thought uneasily.

"I don't need it!" he yelled.

"Sir," Keller snapped in a tone that let one immediately know that what she really wanted to say was "Hey, asshole!" She continued, "What you need is not the issue. This is a court order."

*Don't push him*, Natalie thought. *Let him vent. Bring the level down.*

Crew got up and moved slowly around his desk.

"I don't need it!" the man bellowed, slamming his hand on the desk. "I don't need it." He swiped his hand, knocking the stacking trays to the floor and sending papers flying. "This isn't America. This isn't what I fought for in the war."

"Take it easy," Crew said softly.

"Don't tell me how to take it." His eyes were now bulging, and he inadvertently spit when he said the word 'tell.'

"This meeting is over, sir," Keller said. "You obviously don't care about this probation."

*Ouch!* Natalie thought. *She sounds like his mom. Now it's gonna get ugly.*

"I don't care?! Does it sound like I don't care? I'm a great American." He kicked the desk. "I'm a great American!" His voice broke from the strain. He turned and stormed out. Crew was on his heels, making sure he went directly to the lobby.

"What was his deal?" Wood asked.

Keller picked up her trays and began gathering the papers. Crew returned, bending to retrieve the plastic bottles that had flown to his eighth of the office.

Keller laughed sarcastically. "He doesn't think he needs anger management counseling. Throws his roommate off the second floor balcony...the police come just in time to catch him dragging the guy back up to throw him off again because he wasn't hurt bad enough the first time..."

"That's outrageous," Wood exclaimed. "I say if you don't do it right the first time, you really shouldn't get a second chance."

Crew laughed and added, "Get rid of the condition for counseling and just require him to move to a first floor apartment."

"Doesn't need counseling," Keller grumbled as she pulled her chair with a firm jerk back toward the desk, fighting the worn groves in the carpet.

"He managed not to kill you," Natalie returned with a laugh. "I can't help but admire his restraint after the 'You obviously don't care' remark."

"I know I'm a bitch," she shot back defensively. "The way I look at it, I'm going to be just as nasty as I can be. That way, they won't ever want to be back on probation with me. Maybe they'll think twice before they commit another crime."

"If that logic followed," Natalie returned, "wouldn't you think that someone who went to prison, which, now take no offense, is worse than anything you can dish out, wouldn't you think they'd never commit another crime? But the stats just don't bear out that argument."

Maybe you're right," she said in a dismissive tone that really meant, "You don't know shit."

*Fine*, Natalie thought. There was a time when a tone like that would have really bothered Natalie. But not caring whether or not people agreed with her was one of the few perks of the job. She returned her attention to her pre.

"Agent's description of the Offense," she said softly into the tiny handheld tape recorder.

She reviewed the police report. It was well written, as far as police reports go. It didn't ramble. It was clear to time and place. It had the victim's own words. That was always a touch that Natalie liked to keep in a report, especially when it was a young victim. Sometimes their own terms, filled with fear and insecurity, and sometimes facts that otherwise couldn't be placed in the report, got in under this section. But Natalie knew she had to be careful. Not because of anything that the lawyers or judges would do, but because the typists, the true power in the department of corrections, would start making their own cuts if it was too long. It was a battle Natalie fought, and lost, many times. It didn't matter that the typists had no training in criminal justice, or that their name wasn't the one that would be accountable if the victim showed up to sentencing and found out that the judge got the *Reader's Digest* version of an event that changed their lives forever. Natalie was convinced that some of these typists could turn *War and Peace* into a two-page pamphlet. She went through the report with a black marker and added a few connecting phrases, attempting to keep the impact, but not push the limits of the typist's patience. She returned to her dictation.

"On 12/5/95 at approx. 8:05 p.m., P.O. Gates was dispatched to the Trenton Commons apartments regarding a CSC complaint. Upon arrival, contact was made with complainant Wanda Jackson.

*Information and Belief*

Complainant reported that her 12-year-old daughter had informed her that she had been sexually assaulted. She further reported that the assailant was known to the victim to be Eric James. On 12/6/95, the victim provided the following statement:

"'Eric came over in the morning while my mom was at work. I was home because it was the day after Thanksgiving. He said he knew I was home because his brother and I are in the same class at Trenton Jr. High. I knew I wasn't supposed to let him in, but I did so we could watch videos and stuff. We sat and talked for a while and then he started talking about wanting to have sex. I told him no but he kept telling me it was OK. He unbuttoned and unzipped my pants. He had trouble getting them off me and he yelled at me to take them off. I was scared because he yelled at me so I did. Then he took his hands off and pushed me back on the couch. He started feeling my boobs and told me to take my shirt off. I didn't. He put his hand between my legs and put his fingers in me. I told him it hurt and he said he could make it better. Then he got off me, pushed my legs apart and put his tongue down there. I told him to stop and pulled away. I tried to get up then but he pulled me back down. Then he said, 'Fine, bitch. Just tryin' to help.' Then he got back on top of me and put his penis into me. When he was done he got dressed and acted like nothing happened. When I wouldn't talk to him, he got mad and left.'

"Upon subsequent verbal interview, the victim stated that she had told the suspect, 'I'll call the police if you do it.' When asked re: his response, the victim disclosed that she and the suspect had engaged in consensual sexual intercourse on one occasion. She stated that she had not said anything about this earlier because he said no one would believe her if they knew. She also stated that she was afraid that her mother would blame her if she knew.

"On 12/6/95 at approx. 1:10 p.m., the suspect was contacted by phone and informed of the allegations. He initially denied having known the victim. After being confronted with the fact that other acquaintances would be contacted, he admitted that he knew the victim and that he did have sex with her on several occasions. However, he stated that he believed her to be 17 years of age and that all sexual contact was consensual. He agreed to report to the Trenton PD on 12/7/95 and provide a written statement.

"On 12/7/95 at approx. 9:05 a.m., the suspect contacted this office by phone and stated that, upon the advice of counsel, he would not be making a statement."

"Shit! What the hell did you do?" Green yelled. Natalie turned and saw Green pushing her chair from her desk until she hit the partition, causing it to crash down on the seldom-used desk of Agent Carter. Natalie's gaze went from the fallen partition to the frail-looking woman, then to the desktop. A red puddle toward the center, with a streak leading back to the offender.

"We've got a bleeder," Bradner announced as he bolted from his seat toward the door. "I'll get a supervisor and a spill kit."

"I'll call 911," Keller added.

"What were you thinking?" Green scolded. Having recovered from the initial shock, she repositioned the partition and pulled her chair back up to the desk. "You just can't come in here bleedin' all over the place. We don't know what you got."

"I've done this so many times. I just didn't want to do it again, you know?" The woman was pale, and her speech began to slur. "So I cut the one. Then my dad came to pick me up to come here."

"The ambulance is on the way," Keller said casually as she hung up the phone and returned to her notes.

"Well, they'll be here for you in a minute," Green told her. She opened the file and produced one pink and two white pieces of paper. "We might as well finish up. I need you to sign this release of information on the front and back, then the PA511 program statement and boot camp health questionnaire. Just use the other hand so they don't get all gooied up."

The woman looked dazed. A child lost in a toy store. "What? Sign what?"

"They're just the things we need to finish so we can be done by the time they come for you," Green snapped. "Just sign." She set the papers toward the upper, unbloodied part of the desk.

The woman, holding the bloody wrist to her side, signed all three documents with her good hand while Green held them in place.

"This way," Bradner could be heard saying as he led the paramedics down the hall. He entered with the two-man team and pointed toward the back of the room. "She's right back there." A

*Information and Belief*

crowd of agents began to form at the door, peeking in at the action as the woman was placed on a gurney by one man while the other inspected her wounds before applying direct pressure. She was whisked out.

"How do you think she looks?" Green asked as she disinfected her desk. "She lost a lot of blood. Who knows how long she was bleeding before she got here."

"The answer to your real question is, 'No, you don't have to write the pre if she dies,'" Bradner said as he shook his head and returned to his desk.

"That's not what I meant," she returned defensively.

"That's right," Keller laughed. "Obviously she planned on finishing the report. Why else would she have a woman who was bleeding to death sign forms?"

"Don't be so dramatic. She wasn't dying."

"It's a good thing you were almost done," Natalie added. "You'd really have to tighten that tourniquet if you were only at the family section when she started oozing."

"Oh, stop," Green huffed.

Natalie turned her attention back to her pre. *This will take all day if I don't focus,* she chastised herself. *It's relatively repetitive from here. Just elaborate on the stuff in the Evaluation and Plan.*

"New Paragraph," she continued. "Victim's Impact Statement. The victim of the within...Natalie looked up. Wood entered the room, followed by a young black man wearing a Burger King paper crown. She felt another delay in the making.

"Mr. Stanley," Wood sighed. "Mr. Stanley. I got a call from the FBI." He rubbed his temples. "What are you up to now?"

Stanley threw his head back proudly. "Just reporting a crime."

"Most people call the police for that."

"I've tried the Detroit PD, the Wayne County Sheriff, and the State Police. They all claim to have no jurisdiction in this matter."

Wood decided to move on. "Any police contacts or changes."

"Obviously I've had police contact," Stanley responded impatiently. "I just got done telling you that I've contacted several agencies."

*Ouch*, Natalie thought. *Tactical error. Now you've got to go there.* She glanced over her shoulder and to the right, meeting Wood's desperate eyes. He knew it too.

"OK. What happened."

Stanley pulled a large, flat book from his backpack. "It's all right here," he said, opening the book and turning it to Wood.

He reluctantly took it, first turning the front cover back and reading aloud the title, "*Royal Families.*"

"I got it from the library. I don't even know why I went there that day. It was like something just drew me there. Then I found this book. Then I found the truth."

"The truth?"

"It's right there in front of you."

Wood looked from the book to Stanley. "I'm sorry. You're gonna have to help me out."

"Look at the pictures." His voice raised, taking on a more desperate quality. "The King of the Netherlands. He's my father. Can't you see that?"

"The what?"

"These pictures brought back the memories. The things they thought I'd forgotten. They told me I was born in Alabama to those people who raised me. But I always knew deep down I didn't belong. Now I remember. I was a baby when my mother, the Queen, was driving with me in the car. There was an accident and she got killed. That's when the people who raised me, my foster parents, stole me from there."

"They stole you?"

"They probably didn't mean no harm. But they took me away from the life that by all rights is mine. I told the FBI I didn't want them to go to jail or nothing, but I should get back what's mine. I shouldn't be stuck on the streets when all that stuff is rightfully mine. I should be living the life of a Dutch Royal."

Wood pause, weighing his words. "Mr. Stanley, folks like you and I get mistaken for a lot of things. But there are not too many black Dutch Royals."

Stanley took his book and stared coldly at Wood. "Environment has made me look the way I do." He then glanced around nervously. "There are a lot of people who stand to lose if the story comes out."

*Information and Belief*

He looked down at his book again, then suspiciously at Wood. "And I'm sure they have a lot of people in their pockets."

Wood shrugged and began making notations in his roadbook. "I'm not important enough to be in any pocket, sir. Have you had any other police contact?"

Stanley stood up, fumbling with the pages of his book as he approached Green's desk. "Excuse me. You look like a reasonable person. Do you work here?"

She returned a file to the cabinet and turned to face him. "No, I don't," she responded calmly as she walked past him and out of the room.

He returned to his chair and sheepishly put the book in his backpack.

"Are we done?" Wood asked.

"Yes."

"Any other police contacts or changes."

"No."

"Are you taking your medications?"

Before Natalie could stop it, a laugh escaped her. She was able to catch the last half. *Yeah, right, like clockwork*, she thought. She then cleared her throat and coughed. She knew it wasn't convincing, but she kept her eyes on the page in front of her. Eye contact with anyone was certain to cause a laughing jag that would send this guy right over the edge.

Wood sensed her weakness and moved in for the kill. "Tell me, Mr. Stanley, how do you think the new medication is working out for you?"

*Oh, you bastard!* she thought. *If it were working any better he'd be the King instead of the Prince.* She reverted to the tried-and-true method that kept her clear of the immediate glare, and the future backhand, that laughing in church would guarantee. She bit her knuckle.

Supervisor Kirk entered the bull pen. He glanced uneasily at the young black man in the paper hat before approaching Natalie's desk.

"Fisher, I got a message from…"

"We should really discuss this in your office." She bolted from behind her desk, giving Kirk a gentle push toward the door.

"It's really not that big a…"

"No, really." She pulled him a few feet before he reluctantly followed. She was able to contain her laughter halfway down the hall. When it erupted, Kirk stared at her. She tried to explain when she caught her breath, but ended with a phrase she used frequently since securing employment with the Department of Corrections. "I guess you just had to be there."

He gave a half-hearted, polite chuckle. "Yeah, I guess you would. Anyway, I got a call from court services. They just wanted to confirm that you'd be at the hearing for that guy who went off on Crew."

"Yeah. It's on my calendar. Be there at 9, wait until the judge disposes of everything he thinks is important, wait while he takes a half hour recess, then stand by quietly while the probationer either pleads guilty or the judge continues the guy with the same terms and conditions, after hearing his attorney berate the probation department."

"You'll get that on a good day," he laughed. "But seriously, I think it will go a little harder on him than that. You enter a different area when you start making threats."

"Do you think?"

"This will be his third violation. The only real problem is that he has lifetime probation. Unless the judge sentences him to a prison term, he'll just end up right back here."

"How likely do you think that is?"

"Think about it. A person crazy enough to threaten his probation officer, an authority figure." He noted Natalie's raised eyebrow. "Well, sort of. Anyway, a person like that is dangerous enough to be oblivious to consequences."

"I wonder if the legislature knew what kind of a monster they were creating with lifetime probation. In Wayne County it actually reduces the chance that a guy will get any kind of sanction for violation."

"The funny thing is, I'm sure some clown up there, whoever is taking credit for the idea, is telling people when he campaigns that he's tough on crime and pointing to that as proof."

"What do they think is going to happen in 10 years when we have half the city on paper for a few rocks of crack?"

"It's a paperwork nightmare now. I don't even want to think about what it'll be like in 10 years."

*Information and Belief*

"I think my favorite part is when the guys come in for the pre after pleading guilty. Their lawyers tell them that lifetime is really only five years. Then I tell them I have people reporting from 1987. They about shit, screaming that they're going to withdraw their plea."

"And they always end up coming back. I know. They call me to make sure the agent isn't just making it up."

"That's me," Natalie laughed. "Making stuff up just to rile people."

Kirk looked cautiously around and said in a low voice, "You may be kidding, but we both know there are people who would."

Natalie returned to the bull pen to a chorus of laughter. She smiled and nodded as she returned to her desk. "You know something, Wood? A mature person would just let this go."

"Are you saying what I think you're saying?"

"Exactly. I'll get you. No matter how long it takes. Remember, I lack God-given talent and marketable skills. I'm a civil servant. I'll be here forever. Time is on my side."

"Ooowww," the chorus taunted.

She picked up her Dictaphone, rewound, and listened.

"The victim of the within...She cued the tape at that point and continued, "is Brenda Jackson, age 12 at the time of the offense. She was interviewed by this writer on 12/20/96. She reports that this incident has caused her to miss a significant number of days at school and, ultimately, she had to be removed from classes that she shared with the perpetrator's brother. She reports considerable embarrassment due to the number of people to whom she has had to relay the embarrassing details of this incident. She would also like the court to be aware that she does not believe that justice would be served should the defendant be granted HYTA status. She indicated that the defendant should be reminded of this offense as often as she is.

"New Paragraph. The victim's mother reports that this offense has had a profound effect on the entire family. She states that she worries about the safety of her daughter while she is at work. This, as well as numerous court appearances, has created tensions between herself and her employer. The loss of income has also been a financial hardship to the family. It should be noted that the victim's mother is not requesting restitution. She wants it to be clear that the issue in this matter has nothing to do with money."

Natalie's phone rang. "Probation, Ms. Fisher speaking."
"Hi," Gwen said.
At the sound of her voice, Natalie felt suddenly ashamed. How could she have questioned her loyalty, her love? Natalie could hear it in her voice.
"What time did you get in last night?" Natalie asked.
"I didn't even look. Roger and I didn't even break off until after midnight."
As fast as that, Natalie's suspicions were renewed. She hoped her tone didn't betray the feeling. "What are you two working on?"
"It's complicated. Anyway, I just wanted to let you know that tonight will be late too."
"How late?"
"Probably not as late as last night. But go ahead and have dinner. I'm sure I won't be home in time for that."
"OK," she replied. "I'll see you when you get there."
Natalie hung up. She walked to the drinking fountain. She wasn't thirsty, but she wanted to get away from her desk. The fountain, like most state equipment, worked intermittently. Today was an out-of-order day.
"Fisher, did Kirk remind you about our court date?" Crew asked.
"Huh?"
"Our court date. You know, the guy with all the girlfriends."
Natalie smiled. "You mean Mr. 'There'll be trouble if you come over.'"
"That's him."
"It's on my calendar."
"Good. I've never testified in court. I don't know what to expect."
"It'll be fine," she assured. "Just be sure you bring copies of the warrant and any other documentation you'll need."
"I sent all that stuff down with the file. They'll have it there, right?"
"Do we work for the same department? Come on!"
"Awww, don't scare me like this. It'll be there, right?"

*Information and Belief*

"If you're willing to bet your professional reputation on whether or not inter-office mail will reach the right destination…"

"I get your point," he interrupted. "What can I do now? I already sent it."

"Get a copy of the warrant and supplemental report from your supervisor's file. That way, you'll have all the dates and times and whatnot."

"I never thought about that."

"The last thing in the world you want to tell the judge is, 'He missed about four appointments.'"

## Chapter 35

Natalie grabbed her jacket and exited the back door. Unable to get water from the fountain when she didn't really want it, she suddenly felt a powerful thirst. She also wanted a chance to think. *Gwen's never lied to me. I'm sure there's some other way to explain it. She didn't misspeak, she'd said it was Roger she was working with last night and today. Is she planning some kind of surprise? That's stupid. It's not my birthday or our anniversary. Besides, surprises just aren't Gwen's style.*

She took a Coke out of the cooler, paid, and made her way back to the office. *Wait a minute,* she thought. *Last time I went on vacation, I forgot to change the message for three days.* She noticed for the first time that, despite the sunshine, it was quite cold. The cola in her hand didn't help. She approached the back door but stopped short of punching in the code. *If I go back in now, I'll get swallowed by the insanity and never figure this thing out.* She went to her car and took the phone out of the glove box. *On the other hand, maybe this is the insanity and the stuff in the building is what makes sense. No, it's a combination. The insanity is catching. I was never this paranoid before I worked here.*

She dialed Gwen's number and, after realizing that she had no idea what she was going to say, was relieved when the voice mail greeting invited her to leave a message. She opted against it. *You are soooo paranoid,* she chastised herself as she dialed Roger's number. The message hadn't changed. She had one final idea. She dialed the main number. *This is something I'd expect from an* I Love Lucy *episode after Ricky didn't let her sing at the club.* It then occurred to her that this was incredibly intrusive.

"Advanced Engineering," the receptionist announced.

*Too late to back out.* "This is Lisa Long with the Ford Motor Company. I need to talk to Roger immediately." Natalie's years as an auto worker had taught her that large companies, like Ford, have representatives who treat little companies like dirt. They tend to demand, never ask, to talk to anyone.

*Information and Belief*

"I'm sorry, he's out of the office for the rest of the week. I can put you through to his voicemail or transfer you to the production superintendent."

Natalie rubbed her temple with her free hand. Another possibility down the drain. "I'll call next week," she said curtly, pushing the end button.

A cold burst of air prompted her to mull this over inside. *Why would she lie?* she thought, returning to her desk. *Maybe she's not. Did she say she was working with Roger, or for Roger? Maybe he has her busy on a project while he's away.* But she thought back to both the message and the conversation. Gwen had definitely said "with."

"But you don't understand, child," a kind, but slightly impatient Jamaican voice chided. A middle aged black woman with long dreadlocks sat smiling at Keller. "I'm Rastafarian."

"You're what?" Keller snapped.

"Rastafarian. Smoking the marijuana is a part of my religion, dear. It's a natural thing…"

"I don't want to go over this again. You're finally testing negative. Why are you even bringing this up?"

"Look at me, child. I was never sick a day in my life before you made me go against my religion and nature. Now, I get colds and flu and every other thing that's going around."

"I really can't help that," Keller responded.

"I know you're just doing your job. But I want you to think about it. What if I told you that you couldn't wear that cross around your neck? If you were Catholic and I'd say…"

"I really don't need to hear this."

"So, looks by your reaction that I got it right. What if I said it was against the law for you to take the communion?"

"We're not here to talk about me, ma'am. Did you bring verification of income?"

"I copied my SSI check before I cashed it. They don't come with stubs, you know."

"This will be fine," Keller said flatly, taking the paper.

"Have you heard anything about the travel permit we put in for? My son hasn't had a visitor since the last time I flew down to see him."

"I haven't gotten a response from the court yet. It takes time." She handed a plastic cup and specimen bottle to the woman. "You know," Keller continued, "I was kind of wondering, how does a woman who earns only $400 a month on SSI afford to fly to Texas and back? And all just to visit her son in prison for a few hours."

"Do you have a son?" the woman responded coolly. After waiting for a response, she continued. "I didn't think so. When you have a son taken far away from you, then you'll know how a mother gets the money." She paused and nodding her head concluded, "Any way she can. That's how."

Keller led her from the room.

Natalie rolled through the remainder of her report. It was relatively routine, if not repetitive, from that point. She'd repeat the adult and juvenile record with more detail than was in the evaluation. Just add the docket numbers and dates. Talk a little bit about how he was tossed from place to place as a child. *Probably explains his low opinion of women*, Natalie thought. His drug test had come back negative. Nothing interesting in that section. Work and education were a snap. She put in a couple quotes from his hand-picked therapist for the psychological history section. She noted that she had seen identical quotes from this therapist, referring to each offense as "an anomaly," in his district court and juvenile court record. *How many anomalies make a pattern?* Natalie wondered.

She put the tape in an envelope, sealing it with tape and stapling it to the folder. She'd written an entire report before, only to have the steno lose the tape.

"Can you believe that woman!" Keller fumed. "What an idiot. God, I hate my job."

The combination of Keller's whining about her job, her demeaning comments, and Natalie's sudden insecurity in her own home life caused her to become quickly irritated. "Actually, I thought her argument regarding the constitutionality of the state depriving her of the right to express and practice her well-established religious beliefs was rather insightful."

"Oh, please," Keller moaned.

"Sure," Natalie added sarcastically. "It wasn't nearly as insightful as your 'Oh, please,' but it was worthwhile."

*Information and Belief*

"Well, I guess I just think I know the difference between a religion and a crime. But maybe it's just me," she added in a superior tone that meant, "Just me and anyone else who wants to be right."

Natalie decided this would be a good time to go into the field. It would be way too easy to let this get out of hand. She turned in her report, retrieved her weapon from the lock box, and went to her car.

*That was stupid*, she thought as she drove off. Based on her level of seniority, she'd be in the bull pen with Keller for a good number of years. *That's a long time to sit next to a hostile person.*

She started the car and cranked the heat. It was still sunny, and the snow that had hung on from last week's storm made the light blinding. Natalie dug her aspirin tin out of the glove box and swallowed two with the last of her Coke.

She pulled the folder that contained her client list from her bag. She wasn't sure where she'd go. She didn't really have any pressing need to go anywhere. Policy only required a home call when someone was first placed on your caseload, or if they moved. From that point she could verify the address by talking to family over the phone, or having them bring in mail that had been delivered to their address. But Natalie always exceeded the policy. Partly because she thought it was a good way to get to know offender's families. She'd made a lot of connections that helped at some point down the road with managing cases. But she also did so because she just liked to get out of the office.

She winced when, while putting on the seatbelt, her weapon, still cold from its storage spot in an unheated part of the building, touched her side. She looked at her client list. She had it separated by city, with a reminder on directions noted next to each entry. *Just pick a city*, she thought. She glanced at her watch. It was still relatively early. *Belleville*, she decided. It was the furthest site from the office. *A nice cruise down I-94, the roads should be OK by now.*

The freeway was clear this time of day. She continued to explore her mind for possible explanations for Gwen's lie. But she kept coming back to the one she liked the least. She pulled into the mobile home park off Willis Road. She had three offenders here.

The first was a double-wide with a wooden deck. The gap between the deck surface and the ground was enclosed with lattice work. It had well-maintained shrubs, and the driveway and walk had

*Alexis Janus*

been freshly shoveled. There was no car in the driveway and no light coming from the windows.

She knocked several times and, when there was no response, left one of her cards with a note on the back instructing the probationer to call within 48 hours to verify residence.

The next home was further down the same street. Although the walk hadn't been shoveled, there was a well-beaten path from the steps to the driveway. She walked up the driveway in the tire tracks and then on the path to the door. Again, there was no response. She left her card.

The third was an older model. Natalie saw a cat jet under the home through one of four gaps that resulted from missing skirting. The only impressions in the snow where those left by animals. There was a late-model Ford truck in the driveway. The hood was partially raised, and she could see that snow had gathered on the engine. A piece of plywood had been rested on the back. · Natalie glanced behind it to confirm her suspicions. It was placed there so the expired tags couldn't be seen from the road. As she approached the porch, she noticed that another board was placed over the deteriorated bottom step.

*Shit*, she thought as she tried to kick the snow off her shoes while knocking on the screen. The screen door began to drift toward her. She noticed the catch, which had been held by only one screw, had fallen away by the pressure of her knock. She looked up and saw that the white, icicle-type Christmas lights were still hanging from the gutters. She was amused by the thought that the lights probably doubled the value of the home. She lifted the catch and tried to balance it in place long enough to fasten the door.

She was startled when the inner door flung open. A tall, blond man dressed in a dirty gray sweatsuit leaned against the door jam. "Fisher, c'mon in," he said, stepping out of the door, waving his hand like Vanna White when the little square letters light up. He turned and walked back in before she could respond.

Natalie followed him in, pushing the door until it touched the wall. The glare from the snow made a dim room appear even darker. The first thing that came clearly into focus was a picture of Elvis lacquered to the face of a wooden clock shaped like the state of Michigan. On the far wall, over a couch that was three years past having seen better days, was a tapestry of dogs playing pool. *My God*, Natalie thought, *this is like some caricature of a trailer.*

"Mr. Miller," she said aloud, "I know it's been awhile since I've been out, but it looks like there have been some major changes."

"You might say that," he grumbled, snatching the remote from the top of what, at one time, had likely been some kind of spool for industrial cable, and shutting the television off. "Sandy left. Backed a truck up to the door one day after I left for work and took it all."

"I'm sorry to hear that," Natalie said, thinking, *Do I remember a Sandy?*

"Yep, she took it all. I don't even know where she went," he continued with a tone of sad resignation. "No call, no nothin'. I don't have an answering machine or anything, so I stayed home for three straight days waitin' for the call. But it never came."

"She might still call," Natalie said sympathetically. "How long has it been?"

"Two weeks." His affect seemed at that moment to change for despair to anger. "Did you ever try to get furniture from a garage sale in the winter? Not much available right now. The landlord let me grab a few things out of a trailer that some folks abandoned when they got behind in their rent."

*If this is the stuff he picked out*, Natalie thought, *I'd hate to see what he left.*

He walked into the adjacent kitchen. "Do you want anything?" His tone had made the leap back to cordial.

"No thanks," Natalie said, moving a few more steps in to keep him in her view.

"Oh, lighten up. The day's almost over. Have a beer or something?"

"Excuse me?" Natalie said with confusion. *He didn't just offer me a beer?* she thought. She looked to her right. From this vantage point, she could see a Jack Daniels bottle with about one third of the tea-colored substance remaining. Her mind continued to race. *I don't smell alcohol. But maybe that's why he walked away from the door so quickly, why he's still keeping his distance.*

"It was the goddamned money," he said loudly, overcompensating for the added distance between them.

*God, you're an idiot*, she told herself. *How could you have missed this?*

He stepped toward the sink. "You know what?" His voice had the inflection of an excited child who had thought of something profound for the first time. "You know what?" he repeated as he reached into the sink. "You didn't help one bit. Takin' every last bit of my money right before Christmas."

Natalie didn't like the direction this conversation was taking. "Again," she said, "I'm very sorry. When I see you next week we can…"

"That's right," he yelled. "Fuck up my life and don't even hang around to listen."

Natalie went cold. As he stepped back from the sink, she saw that he had a knife in his hand. "You don't care about me or my life. You just want your fucking money!"

Natalie's brain raced. *What's he doing? He's not moving toward me. But it would only take a second. How far am I from the door? About three seconds. Closing it after me would give me a few more seconds to beat him to my car. Did I lock it? Key's in my pocket. Rummaging through all that shit will take time.* She could hear the instructor's megaphoned voice from handgun training. "From the holster, you have four seconds. Draw and shoot two rounds in four seconds…watch your sights…" She unsnapped her coat, then remembered her mace was in her right pocket. Then remembered that, when she was instructed to spray her canister empty before turning it in for her yearly refill, it had been a dud. *No time to try something new if that doesn't work.*

"What did you get for Christmas?" he yelled.

*Give instruction*, she remembered. *Keep your voice steady. Be firm. Don't let him know you're about to shit.* She took a breath. "Mr. Miller," she said flatly, "put the knife down."

"What?" he asked. He looked at the knife as though it were some foreign object. "Oh, please," he sneered, tossing it back to the sink. "I was just gonna put it in the dish washer. I got stuff to do. If you don't want to watch, then maybe you should just go."

Natalie took two steps back as he reentered the room and flopped back on the couch. He picked up the bottle. "Alcohol's not illegal, you know." He retrieved the remote and clicked the television on. "Unless you want to watch Springer, I think you should go."

Natalie needed no further prompting. She took a last glance at the large man, now transfixed by women fighting on a stage while spewing a flurry of insults between beeps inserted a half a second too late to truly render the profanity inaudible. He seemed unflustered, unaware that he had taken Natalie through a process that no simulator or training ever could. In that moment, that split second before he had thrown the steak knife in the sink, she had drawn a mental line at the point where the linoleum met the carpet. If he had passed that point with the knife, she was going to shoot him.

This thought left her shaken and exhausted. But more than anything, it left her wanting to talk. Not to anyone at work. It wouldn't look very good to tell another agent that she had been ready to blow a guy away for loading the dishwasher in a hostile manner. This was not the touchy-feely world of social work, where processing experiences was encouraged. The slightest acknowledgment of vulnerability could turn her into the office joke. Telling a family who thought the job was too dangerous to start with would make Christmas hell for the next three years or so. She needed to talk to Gwen.

She headed for home.

As she turned into her driveway, she was determined to make a pot of coffee and wait up for Gwen. But the note on the table froze her in her tracks for the second time that day.

> *Had to go to Cincinnati for the weekend. I should be back Sunday night. This project is getting bigger all the time. Tried to call, but you were out. I won't get in until late tonight, so I'll call tomorrow.*
>
> *Miss You,*
> *Gwen*

## Chapter 36

Natalie didn't sleep that weekend. At each attempt, she was awakened by the sound of Gwen's voice saying, "I'm working late with Roger," or the sight of Mr. Miller, the Jack Daniels bottle, and the knife.

True to her word, Gwen called twice. On Saturday, Natalie went to the grocery store and missed the first one. The message left did not name a hotel, or a number Gwen could be reached at. Natalie took the portable phone with her around the house for the rest of the day. Toward the evening, she remembered Mr. Miller saying that he had stayed home for days waiting for his girlfriend to call. *Oh God*, she thought, *I'm becoming one of them.*

On Sunday, she didn't wait. Her eyes still blurry from lack of sleep, she went out to get a paper. When she got back, there was a message from her mother reminding her that she still had a family. The second message was from Gwen. "I'll be landing at Metro at about 11 tonight. By the time I take the shuttle to long term parking and finally get out of there, it'll be pretty late. God, I'm tired. Anyway, I guess I'll see you Monday night."

Natalie was torn. On one hand, she wanted to stay up. This was making her crazy. On the other hand, she was as tired as she had ever been. A situation like this could get way out of hand. She didn't want to believe that Gwen was seeing someone else, but she also couldn't come up with another answer. Was that because her brain was sleep deprived? *You can't just come right out and ask her*, she thought. *I'll have to ask her something, but I don't want to sound like I'm accusing her. Maybe I should try to take a nap.* Then she remembered the dreams that had startled her awake a half dozen times last night, most of them ending in her shooting Mr. Miller. He lay on the floor bleeding, and she'd walked over to find that what was a knife when she'd shot was now large wooden cooking spoon.

*I know*, her brain screamed at her. *Call Robin.*

They had been best friends in high school but had not come out to each other until almost five years later. Afterward, they frequently laughed at how blind the other had been.

*Information and Belief*

"Christ," Robin would grin, "I had posters of Farrah Fawcett and Kate Jackson all over my room. How could you not have known?"

"At least you were dating guys," Natalie replied. "I was no cover girl, but did it occur to you that I probably could have landed at least a geekie date if I'd wanted one?"

But in the end, they agreed that they had both likely missed all the signs because they hit too close to home. They had both been far too busy trying to convince themselves that they were normal.

After the second ring, a voice said, "Hello."

Natalie recognized it as Robin's lover, Jill. "Hi Jill, it's Natalie."

"Well hi," she repeated in a cheery tone. "How have you been?"

"Not bad," she lied. "And you?"

"Busy. We're just getting ready to start rehearsal. You know we're going to be playing the bar circuit next month. Robin's such a perfectionist," she groaned.

"Tell me about it," Natalie laughed, remembering the hours her friend spent in her basement, unwilling to leave until "it's right."

"Well, let me get her for you. The drummer hasn't shown up yet, so we've got a few minutes."

"Thanks," Natalie said.

She could hear Robin tuning her guitar. The sound of footsteps, voices, and more footsteps was followed by, "Well, hello stranger!"

"Hey, how ya been?"

"Busy. Did Jill tell ya we're playing the bars next month?" She continued before Natalie could respond. "It'll be good to get out again. I didn't realize how much I missed it until we started practicing again. The moral of this story is, never break up with your drummer…"

"Unless the base player is really good looking," Natalie finished with a laugh.

Robin laughed even harder. "Yeah, all in all, I guess it was worth it. I can always find a new drummer."

"Hey, that reminds me. This guy at my office, he's in a band and the other day he asked me an interesting question."

"What?" Robin asked, hoping it would be on her favorite category, music trivia.

"What do you call a person who hangs out with musicians?"

"What?"

"The drummer."

"Oowww. That's cold. You're lucky you didn't say that one in front of Connie. They'd have found your body by the side of the road with a drum stick through your heart."

"My probationers would say that's impossible. I have no heart."

"Shit," Robin teased. They're probably right. So, what's up?" she asked, changing tone quickly. "I've known you long enough to know that the self-abasing humor means something."

"You're good. You really should have been a shrink."

"Lucky for you I'm not. You'd have racked up quite a bill over the years."

"I suppose so."

"OK," Robin said. Natalie could hear her light a cigarette. "The doctor's in. What's up?"

"Nothing, I hope," she began.

She spilled the whole story, describing each call and every option she had considered. "So," she concluded, "what do you think?"

Robin took a long drag on her cigarette, and Natalie could hear it being ground out in the ashtray. "She's cheating on you."

Natalie's heart sank. "Do you really think that's a possibility?"

"No," Robin responded sternly. "I didn't say it was a possibility. I said she's cheating on you."

"You don't see any other possibilities?"

"Look," Robin said sympathetically. "I know this isn't what you want to hear, but you also know that's way you called me. You know I'm gonna be straight with you. Are there other possibilities? I'm sure there are if we look hard enough. Do I think they're right? No. My gut tells me that the most obvious answer is right."

"I was kind of afraid of that." Natalie could hear doors slamming, and raised, friendly voices in the background. "Sounds like your drummer showed up."

"Yeah, that's her," Robin confirmed. "You know, we'll only be playing for a few hours. Do you want to come over for dinner?"

"No thanks. Maybe some other time."

"Are you sure? We don't have to do dinner. We could just hang out or…"

"No, really. I appreciate it. But I think I'll just take a nap and wait up for Gwen."

"Well, call me if you need to. You know I'm usually up late, so whatever time, just give me a shout."

"Thanks," Natalie said. "I'll call if I need to."

As she hung up, the cat jumped on her lap and walked in circles, his tail hitting Natalie's nose three times before he settled into her arms. "After all these years, Rowdy, your timing is still perfect."

She stroked the purring tabby and fought back the urge to cry. In spite of all her social work training, she still hated to cry. Her gut reaction was that it was weak. Although she felt she could accept weakness in others, she was filled with self-loathing at the idea of giving in to it for herself. Her practical, educated side found this amusing. "Nothing wrong with you that a good 10 years of therapy wouldn't cure," she said aloud.

She lay down on the sofa, the cat quickly settling into a new position against her. The thought of starting again, maybe having to move, meeting new people, was overwhelming.

She closed her eyes. In what seemed like only a few moments, she saw Mr. Miller. She was back in his living room. He was yelling, appearing more menacing than before. Instead of a steak knife, he had a large butcher knife. He came toward her. He crossed her mental line of no return. She pushed her coat back and gripped her weapon, her thumb unsnapping the thumb brake perfectly, just like in training. While doing so, as she had been trained, she yelled, "Probation officer, stop!" with full knowledge that he wouldn't. She pointed at center mass and pulled on the trigger. It wouldn't budge. She pulled again. Nothing. The knife was raised and almost over her head. The trigger wouldn't budge.

She bolted up and off the couch before she realized that she was still in her front room. She searched the house, finding the cat cowering under the bed. "Sorry about that, baby," she said soothingly as she pulled Rowdy out. She hugged her close and kissed her on the back of the head. "It's OK. It's going to be OK."

# Chapter 37

The up side to the nightmares for Natalie was that she would have no trouble waiting up for Gwen. It was 12:45 a.m. when she saw the headlights sweep through the front and then the side windows. She felt a little panicky as she heard Gwen lock the car door, open the trunk, and remove what must have been her bag and briefcase.

*How are you going to start?* she wondered. *What do you say first?*

Gwen was fumbling with her keys. Natalie walked over and unlocked and opened the door.

Gwen gasped. Then, realizing it was Natalie, she let out a sigh of relief. "You scared the hell out of me."

Natalie opened the storm door. Gwen, holding a suitcase in one hand, her briefcase under the same arm, and toting a garment bag over the other shoulder, with her fingers gripped to the tops of the hangers, entered. She threw the garment bag over a chair as Natalie took the briefcase out from under her arm and laid it next to the couch. Gwen dropped the suitcase to the floor after kicking the door closed behind her. Then she took Natalie into her arms.

Natalie felt as though she was melting into this hug. Like it was the first or best hug she'd ever had. For that moment, all suspicion was gone. A person who could hold her like this couldn't possibly be holding anyone else. She couldn't possibly have this much left.

"What are you doing up this late?" Gwen asked as she pulled away.

"I missed you."

"Me, too," she replied.

The tone was a bit too casual for Natalie's liking. Like a cobra, suspicion struck, digging its fangs deep into Natalie's soul. Everything in her mind said, *No, not now. It's late. You're tired. This isn't the time.*

"Gwen," Natalie started, unable to hold the thought any longer, "I know you weren't working with Roger last week."

"What?" she asked, walking into the bedroom.

Natalie followed. "I know you weren't working late last week." Her voice was flat, reflecting the lack of energy that she felt. "Where have ya been?"

Gwen took her nightshirt out of the top drawer and turned to face Natalie. "What are you talking about?" she asked defensively. "I was working with…"

"No you weren't," Natalie interrupted softly. She had made up her mind. She wasn't going to argue specifics. That was a trap. She'd learned from felons that getting into times, dates, and quotes put you into an endless loop.

"I don't know…"

"Yes you do, Gwen. You know." She rubbed her burning eyes. "Just tell me. I need to know."

Gwen looked down at her hands, which were now pulling the collar of her shirt out of shape. "I can tell you that it's not what you think."

Natalie sat on the bed. "Then tell me what to think."

Gwen sat next to her. "I didn't tell you because I knew you probably wouldn't like it. But I'm not cheating."

Natalie felt instantly relieved, and even a little energized. This was coming to an end. She could hear the truth in Gwen's voice, and now this was almost over.

"OK. Just tell me what's been going on."

"It started a few months ago. Some people in the office went out for drinks after work. There's been this one guy, Bob, I've always known that he likes me, but that night, he was being really obvious." She ran her fingers through her hair. "Well, I went into the lady's room and a few of the others started commenting on how good looking he was and pointing out that he was single. At first I just told them that I'm not really in the market right now. You know, the old, I'm-focused-on-my-career-right-now excuse. But then one person mentions that I never seem to be dating anyone, then someone else asks in this snide way if there isn't really another reason that I'm not dating." At that point, she stopped talking and unbuttoned her shirt.

"And then what?" Natalie asked.

Gwen pulled her nightshirt over her head. "Then nothing."

Natalie was growing impatient. "Nothing doesn't keep you out all night," she said sternly.

Gwen's eyes widened for a moment. Natalie rarely raised her voice, and it caught Gwen off guard. "I've been going to places, certain events that I know I'll be seeing coworkers at. I'm not sleeping with him or anything. I just need to distract the busybodies at work who have nothing better to do than to keep track of that kind of thing." She moved next to Natalie, putting her arm around her shoulder. "I would never cheat on you," she concluded, gently kissing her on the cheek.

Natalie could feel her own tears rolling down her face. She got up and quickly brushed them away. "You've been dating a coworker for months and lying about where you were. What do you call that?"

"I'm just…"

"I know," Natalie interrupted. "Your just so ashamed to be with me that you had to invent a whole other life to show the world. Do you really think that's supposed to make me feel better?"

"Look," Gwen pleaded. "Just because I don't want to wear a sign that says I'm a lesbian doesn't mean that I don't love you. I've got to work. It would be career suicide to let them know I'm gay."

"You've worked on Wall Street and got your MBA from one of the most prestigious schools in the country. Do you really expect me to believe that you'd be out pumping gas somewhere if this company decided they couldn't tolerate a dyke in their midst?"

Gwen began to cry. "You don't understand that part of me. You never have. Doesn't it bother you that people who don't even know who you are hate you? I've told you about my friend Rita. She's a great person and I really like her. But she's also born again. I've heard the way she talks about gays." Her sobs were interrupting the flow of her speech. "If she knew…she'd still…she'd still be nice, but…it wouldn't be the same."

"I just can't understand why you'd want to be friends with someone who'd hate you if she knew who you really were? Is that person really a friend in the first place?"

"Yes," Gwen sobbed. "That's what you don't get. Yes. She's my friend. She's important. What other people think is important."

Natalie took her nightwear out of the dresser, slamming the drawer. "You say I don't understand you, and maybe you're right. But it's real clear that you don't understand me. I see dating someone else, for any reason, as cheating. Sex isn't required to betray a relationship." Natalie walked to the door. "You need to think about what's really important to you. If I'm going to always come in second...with the person you want the world to think you are coming in first...well, I can't take that. I won't be able to live with that."

Natalie took her pillow and the top blanket off the bed and went out to the couch. Gwen offered no protest. She set the small alarm on her pager and turned off the light.

## Chapter 38

Natalie handed the parking attendant $5. He stuck an orange stub under the windshield wiper and pointed to the back of the lot. Normally, she would have parked in the structure. It was cheaper and the car would be covered. But normally she wouldn't have spent the night on the couch, catching catnaps between nightmares, before coming to court.

She pulled down the visor and slid back the tiny door that covered the mirror. She looked tired, her eyes were a little red around the edges. She slid the door closed, deciding that she'd looked worse on better days.

She put her hands in her jacket pockets, remembering that she'd left her gloves on the counter. The wind had kicked up and it had started to snow. Not the nice, big flakes that she had loved as a kid. The ones that fell when it was just warm enough to make for good packing snow. The kind that snowmen and forts were made of. Today it was the fine snow that came down in the bitter cold. The kind that keeps blowing, unaffected by the loads of salt that the city futilely dumped on the ground. It hadn't been bad coming in, but it was going to be a tricky drive back.

She kicked the snow off her feet on the carpet of the entrance to the Frank Murphy Hall of Justice. She entered through the exit door, showing her badge and identification to the security guard. Not having to wait in line at the metal detectors was one of the few perks the agents had in the court system.

She waited in front of one of the four elevators that serviced the entire building. She'd learned that it was best to pick one and wait. Trying to shift to the first one that opened was usually an experience that she imagined would be very much like a fish trying to jump up Niagara Falls, lots of effort just to end up beating yourself to death on the rocks. She watched as the mini-bedlam broke out after each door opened. Attorneys, gang members, and jurors, the latter always identifiable by the blue tags with the word 'Juror' slapped on their Sunday best, pushed their way into the cars.

*Information and Belief*

When the door before her opened, she stepped in and to the right. She was only going up to the 5th floor. She didn't want to get trapped behind the crowd.

To her surprise, Crew walked in behind her. "Hey," she said. "Good morning. I didn't notice you out there."

Crew smiled. "I got lucky. The door opened just as I came around the corner. I was able to slide right in. Think it's a good omen?"

"We can only hope. Did you make a duplicate file?"

"Right here," he responded, tapping his briefcase. "Glad you suggested it."

The door opened to their floor and they excused their way past the other irritable occupants.

"Wow, too bad about Elds." Crew had stopped short of the courtroom, taking off his gloves and overcoat.

"What about her?"

"Didn't you hear? She had to put her house up for sale."

"You're kidding!"

"No. I heard that she's going to take a real beating on it, too. She has to unload it quick before she loses it outright for not making the mortgage."

"That's incredible."

As Crew held opened the courtroom door, Natalie saw a familiar face pass by. She stopped, watching the young woman walk down the hall toward another courtroom. She thought for a second, then remembered the name. Sophia. Eric James' girlfriend. The girl joined Eric, and a man Natalie assumed must be his attorney.

"Someone you know?" Crew asked.

Natalie followed Crew into the courtroom. "I wrote the pre on that guy."

The courtroom was quiet. There was one deputy sitting in front of a computer, and another sitting in a chair by the box where the in-custody defendants are held.

"Nice touch," Natalie continued. "Has his little girlfriend wearing maternity wear. There's no way she's even showing yet."

Crew laughed. "Gotta show the judge that mouth to feed."

"When I was in child welfare, I was working with this family, I think the original complaint was environmental neglect or something, anyway the dad had a record that would stretch halfway across the room. But he never got any time. When I asked him why, he pointed to his son. This kid's in a wheelchair and brain damaged due to a car accident. This guy parades his handicapped son like a show pony in front of the judge for sympathy. And it works."

"That's sick."

"It gets better. The thing is, he's the one who put this kid in the chair. Driving drunk one night. Got into a fight with his wife, roughs her up, then takes the baby with him out of spite, tellin' her he's leaving and she'll never see her son again. Throws the infant on the passenger side, no infant seat. Didn't even try to fasten the kid in at all. Like a sack of potatoes. When he smashes the car up on a tree, the kid almost dies, and of course, not a scratch on our man."

A few people began to filter into the courtroom. Attorneys wandered in, called a name, and took clients they had never met before into a hallway, usually advising them to plead guilty to a lesser charge. Occasionally, a shout of protest could be heard.

The court-appointed probation officer, or CAPO as they were commonly known, was nowhere in sight. In most court systems, probation officers do their own hearings. But in a county as large as this it would be impossible, considering that the agents were housed in five different offices in different parts of the city. It was also unnecessary, as most probationers pled guilty to the violation when they learned that they would just be warned and placed back on probation anyway. The agent who supervised the case was only called when the probationer wanted a hearing because he believed that he might actually go to jail.

"Where is he with that file?" Crew said nervously as the court clerk and recorder took their seats.

"Relax," Natalie said. She looked around. The room was beginning to fill up. The court system of old, where defendants wore suits, was long gone. Baggy jeans, bandanas, and $100 running shoes made up the bulk of the wardrobes. The jackets were reserved for the lawyers, detectives, and probation officers. Natalie noted that one clean-cut white male in the back row was wearing a suit. *Sex offender*, she thought.

"All rise," a deputy announced as the judge entered and briskly took his seat.

*Information and Belief*

"Donavan, docket 96-8987, come forward." The clerk, a fair-skinned black woman with oversized glasses, continued to sort papers while the attorney signaled for his client. A short black man who had to weigh in at more than 350 pounds slowly lumbered to the front.

"Your Honor, Jerry Dailey on behalf of my client, Mr. Clarence Donavan."

The prosecutor stood. "John Dane for the People. The parties have reached an agreement, Your Honor. At this time, we ask that count 1," he glanced at the yellow legal pad, "felonious assault, be dismissed, and the defendant will plead guilty to count 2, misdemeanor assault and battery."

"Is this correct?" the judge asked.

"Yes, Your Honor. At this time my client is willing to plead guilty to the simple assault."

The judge looked wearily upon the defendant. "Mr. Donavan, is it your intent to plead guilty to count 2, assault and battery, at this time?"

The obese young man looked at his attorney. After observing the nod he awaited, he replied, "Yes."

The judge, obviously bored with this part of the proceeding, mindlessly rattled off, "Has anyone promised you anything in exchange for this plea?"

"No."

"Has anyone made any promises to you regarding the sentence?"

"No."

"Do you understand that by pleading guilty you have given up your right to a jury trial, a right to question witness against you and call witnesses on your behalf?"

The young man looked at his attorney, who nodded. "Yes."

"Then you are pleading guilty today because you are, in fact, guilty and not as a result of any promise or threat."

"Yes."

"Very well. The plea is accepted. State for the record, the facts of the assault."

He looked at his attorney.

"Briefly, and I emphasize, briefly, tell us what happened."

"I hits my sister wit a bat."

Crew leaned and whispered, "Can you believe they're letting him off with a misdemeanor for beating someone with a bat?"

"The sister was probably a reluctant witness," Natalie explained. "They were lucky to get him on anything."

"We request that bond be continued until the time of sentencing," the defending attorney stated.

"No objection," the prosecutor added.

"Bond continued," the judge agreed. "Mr. Donavan, you will need to go directly to the probation building for the scheduling of a pre-sentence report. Return here for sentencing on..." the judge looked at the clerk.

"March 3rd," she said.

"March 3rd," he repeated and tapped his gavel.

The clerk took the next file from the top of what Natalie now noticed to be a large pile. "Get comfortable," she whispered to Crew.

And on it went. Charges were read, pleas to something substantially less serious were offered and accepted, and instructions to return for sentencing were provided.

At 11:45, the CAPO, Alan Richards, entered the room. He motioned for Natalie and Crew to met him in the hall.

"What was your guy's name again?" he asked. Just then, he did a double take. "On second thought, here." He handed Crew the stack of files he was carrying. "I need to catch up with that guy."

Before Crew could ask a question, he was gone around the corner. "He'll be a big help," Crew muttered as he shuffled the files. "Mills, here we are."

"The file. Bonus," Natalie said.

"I'm so glad to see this. I made the copies you told me to make, but I didn't copy my actual notes." He put his hand to his heart. "I feel so much better."

Richards returned and Crew handed back the remaining files. "Are all of these cases going today?" Crew asked.

"Yeah, but don't worry. Most will plead out. The ones that don't will be set for hearing on another day."

"It's almost 12. Is he going to break for lunch? I'm starved."

"I doubt it," Richards responded. "He may take a 10-minute recess and have a bagel, but it won't be long enough for you to get anything."

"He works right through until 5?"

Richards laughed. "Let me put it to you this way. If you're on a scavenger hunt and have a judge on your list, this is the last place in the world you'd want to look after 3:30. Down here, most courts start at 10:30 and end at 3."

"Speak of the devil," Crew said, looking past Natalie.

She turned and recognized the little man, along with an elderly couple that Natalie assumed to be the parents, and a young, blond female in a blue suit. Natalie recognized her as an attorney she had seen several times. Although not in a suit, the defendant was neatly dressed in a pair of Dockers, white shirt, and a sweater vest.

"Why is it I'm always told to be in court at 9?" Natalie asked in frustration. "The attorneys roll in by 9:45, the judge around 10:30, and it never fails the felon wanders in whenever he wants. You know darn well if we were two minutes late we'd be in contempt."

"Yeah," Crew agreed. "Sometimes I think I'm the only sucker in the world who still wakes up to an alarm."

Richards returned, and Crew pointed out the defendant.

"Great," Richards said. "Come with me and maybe we can settle this thing before we go in."

"Oh, that would be great." Crew was smiling now, and seemed relieved at the prospect of avoiding a hearing.

The blond spotted Richards, motioned for the defendant and his family to enter the court, and met Richards in the middle. Her purposeful pace and stern demeanor sent an instant signal to Natalie. Nothing was going to get settled out here. Natalie looked at Crew. He was still smiling.

"Ms. Smith," Richards greeted warmly. "How have you been?"

"Fine," she replied with little enthusiasm. "So, do you want to try and explain what's going on here?"

Richards, sensing the mood, made his own shift. "What's going on is a hearing for violation of probation. I'm pretty sure that's written on the warrant request."

Crew looked like a kid who'd just been told there's no Santa. He gave Natalie a panicked look before regaining his composure.

"Look, we both know this is a petty technical violation. I can probably get my guy to plead if you're going to recommend continued probation."

"I didn't drive all the way downtown just to recommend that everything stay the same. It makes all the time and effort seem a little silly, don't you think?" Crew said defensively.

"Not nearly as silly as this warrant." She turned, facing him directly. "And not nearly as silly as you might look when we get in front of the judge."

Crew's face was emotionless. "I'll chance it." He used a tone that left Natalie thinking that his next line would be, "Bond, James Bond."

"Then we'll see you in front of the judge." She turned and walked curtly into the courtroom.

"Where'd he get the money to hire Perry Mason?" Crew asked angrily.

"You're dating yourself. I'd go with Johnny Cochran or Marsha Clark," Natalie suggested.

"Shit. A petty technical violation," he said, imitating the voice and posture of the attorney. "I guess not knowing where this guy lives is just technical. Can you imagine how people would scream if this guy committed some big-time crime while he was on probation? When they found out we weren't even sure where he lived, they'd have my head."

"Or if they found out he was making threats to you and you took no action," Natalie added. "If he goes out and kills someone and the media finds out he was demonstrating violent behavior right in front of his PO, you're on the front page tomorrow."

"Let's get back inside," Richards said with a wave of his hand that reminded Natalie of a wagon train leader in an old western movie.

They sat through four more pleas. In each case, the defendant's rights were fully explained. In each case, they were directed to the probation building. Natalie knew from experience that at least half would blow it off and claim the judge never told them anything about a probation appointment or a pre-sentence report.

The clerk gave Richards a nod, which prompted him to approach with the large stack of files.

"Let's move this along," the judge said impatiently.

"Violators," the clerk responded before announcing, "Calling case 94-009878, Davis. 95-012230, Jabowski. 96-008908, Roland. 95-011213, Albert. 96-008769, Finny. All approach."

*Information and Belief*

Three men went forward from the gallery. Two in county jail orange were led from the custody bench set off to the right of the courtroom. Two well-dressed females and one elderly man, in a suit wrinkled enough to convince Natalie that he must have slept in it, approached the bench, working their way between the row of defendants.

The wrinkled suit was the first to speak. "Andrew Barns on behalf of…" He held the file forward and at arms length. "On behalf of defendants Jabowski and Roland."

"Angelia McCabe on behalf of defendants Davis and Finny."

"Bella Manella on behalf of Mr. Albert."

"Alan Richards for the probation department." He opened the top file and read from the supplemental report written by any one of the hundreds of agents in the county. "Docket 94-009878, Dante Davis. The defendant tested positive for cocaine twice and refused to provide a sample when instructed on three occasions."

"Man, you try to take a leak with some burley dude crowdin' yo back," the first young man protested.

The judge looked disapprovingly toward him as his attorney nudged him with her elbow.

"How do you plead?" the judge asked, his attention temporarily diverted by a sudden need to sort the papers on his desk.

The attorney looked at the defendant and nodded.

"Guilty," he grumbled.

"Next," the judge prompted as he tapped the papers on their bottom edge and into perfect alignment.

"95-012230, Donald Jabowski." Richards ran his finger down the center of the page, his lips moving slightly before he said aloud, "Failure to report."

"Plea?" The judge had now abandoned his papers and had moved on to joining the remaining clips.

Crew leaned toward Natalie and whispered, "I spend an hour writing a supplemental report to send with the warrant and some guy like Richards ends it with three words."

"Guilty," Jabowski said.

"Next," the judge said without looking up.

"Docket 96-008908, Dale Roland. Walked out of inpatient substance abuse treatment."

"Plea?"

The slender, blond man lean toward his attorney, whispering as the man in the wrinkled suit shook his head vehemently.

"Plea," the judge repeated impatiently.

More whispering. The wrinkled suit relented. "Your Honor," he said wearily, "the defendant would like to plead guilty with an explanation."

The judge sighed and looked at his watch. "Quickly."

The wrinkled suit nodded to the defendant.

"Your Honor, a week after I entered rehab, I called my cousin and he told me that the roofer he works for needs help. I was already clean. It's not like I've got some out-of-control drug problem. I got busted using a little coke with some friends. It was a one-time thing. Your Honor, I can understand some kind of fine or something. But society doesn't benefit when I'm not working."

"Did you bring a check stub to verify that employment?"

"I get paid cash."

"Then I guess when you say society benefits, you don't mean the Internal Revenue Service. You'll leave the bill for needed city services for someone else."

A few people in the back chuckled. The wrinkled suit ran his hand nervously through his comb-over.

"And you're telling me that you've been clean since the time you left rehab," the judge continued.

The young man sensed his opportunity. "Yes, Your Honor. That was a one-time thing. I swear, if you give me this chance…"

"I'll do you one better," the judge interrupted. "We can send you right downstairs. We have a drug testing unit that can give us instant results. Deputy, please escort the defendant."

The blond's expression, once hopeful, now resembled that of a deer in the headlights. The deputy approached.

"Is there something you'd like to tell me before we spend the county's money on this test?" the judge asked.

The blond's eyes pleaded to the wrinkled suit. The wrinkled suit shook his head in disgust.

"Is there something you'd like to tell us before you run up your tab, sir?" the judge said sternly.

"It'll be dirty," he mumbled.

*Information and Belief*

"Guilty plea accepted. Next."

"Docket 95-011213, Dennis Albert."

"Guilty," the middle-aged man in county orange blurted out.

More chuckles from the back.

The judge smiled. "That's the pace I'm looking for. Next."

"Docket 96-008769, Alvin Finny."

"Yeah, I'z guilty too yo' honor," the young, black man in county orange said contemptuously. "We awl guilty."

"Very well. All probations continued with same terms and conditions." He tapped his gavel. "Anything left?" he asked the clerk.

"We've got one probation violation hearing."

"Twenty minute recess," he called as he bolted to his feet and walked quickly to his chambers.

## Chapter 39

Natalie dumped the last of her change into the pay phone.
"This is Gwen."
"Hi," Natalie said, sounding more tentative than she had planned.
"Hi."
"I missed you this morning. What time did you leave?"
"I don't know. Early."
"I noticed that some of your things were missing from the bathroom. What are you…"
"This really isn't a good time," Gwen said, in a voice straining to remain calm.
"Well, if you're gonna take your stuff, it doesn't sound like there's gonna be a good time."
"Look, I've been thinking about this for a long time," she said quietly. "I can't give you what you want."
Natalie felt a tingling sensation run down from her face and through her body. "What do you mean?"
"You know what I mean. I don't know why being right up in people's faces is so important to you, but I can't do it."
"You mean you won't do it."
"You are exasperating! Our life is our business. Why is this so important to you?"
"Because being a couple is like being a team. It's us against the world. I expect you to side with me, not with the world."
"I was with you."
"Was?"
"Look," Gwen said softly. "I can't talk now."
"I know that tone," Natalie said bitterly. "Someone just came into the room."
"Yeah."
"No problem. Just tell 'em you're arguing with your boyfriend." Natalie winced when she heard the abrupt click on the other end.
"Fisher," Crew called, leaning out the door of the court. "We're back in session."
Natalie quietly returned to her place next to Crew on the bench.
"Case 89-3250, Bruce Mills."

Richards nodded to Crew and Natalie. They passed through the small swinging hinged door built into the partition that separated the spectators from the participants. Natalie stood between Richards and Crew. The defense attorney took her place next to Richards. The defendant stood on the other side of her, looking nervously at the elderly couple that remained on the benches.

*Maybe not parents. Maybe grandparents*, Natalie thought.

The blond attorney spoke first. "Angela Smith, on behalf of Mr. Mills."

"Alan Richards for the probation department."

"Natalie Fisher for the probation department."

"Henry Crew for the probation department."

"This is a violation of probation hearing, Your Honor." Richards looked at the supplemental report and began reading. "On December 20th of last year, the probationer called the supervising agent and…"

"Hold on a minute," the blond interrupted. "Your Honor, are we going to swear in and call witnesses?"

"This is an informal hearing, Ms. Smith. Proceed."

Richards tried again. "On December…"

"I'm sorry, Your Honor," Smith said. "But I don't think a monologue by a person who didn't witness the incident in question is really appropriate, when we have the supervising agent right here."

*She's good*, Natalie thought. *She must have senses, or maybe researched, to find the weak link.*

The judge sighed. "Fine, let's just move along."

Crew, following Richards' cue, began to read from his supplemental report. "On December…"

"Your Honor," Smith burst in, "why is he reading from a report? Does he know what happened or not?"

"It's his report," Richards countered. "Why can't he present the report he wrote?"

The judge slapped his hand on the bench. "Address the questions to me, not each other," he chastised. "Ms. Smith," he continued, "it is perfectly appropriate for Mr. Crew to read his report. It is, after all, his written account of what happened. But I will add," he said as he turned his attention to Crew, "I have had a chance to review your report. Feel free to tell me what happened. The dates and times are already included in your warrant request."

Crew, feeling more at ease, fell into his story. "The defendant has a poor reporting record. So,..

"Your Honor," Smith interrupted, "what constitutes a poor reporting record?"

The judge shook his head impatiently. "Ms. Smith, please let this young man finish."

Natalie could tell that this minor defeat for the defense gave Crew enhanced confidence. "Your Honor, the defendant called and told me he couldn't come in because he hurt his leg and he couldn't get out. Then I heard the traffic behind him and he admitted that he was calling from a phone booth."

The judge smiled and nodded.

"Then he became angry because I told him if he could make it to the phone booth, he could make it the rest of the way to the office. When he got to the office, he started ranting about living with one girlfriend, but having another drive him around. Anyway, I told him I would have to make a home visit to confirm that he moved. Then he started talking about being on medication and not being held responsible for his actions if I came out."

"And what exactly does that mean, Your Honor?" Ms. Smith cut in. "It could mean any number of things. My client could have meant that he loses track of time due to his medications and may forget the appointment. He could have…"

"Point taken," the judge said with a wave of his hand. "Mr. Crew, was he threatening you?"

"Absolutely, Your Honor. There's not a doubt in my mind."

"Your mind is not the issue here," Smith said.

"Counsel," the judge admonished, "I asked a question. I don't expect you to tear this man apart for answering it."

"I'm sorry, Your Honor."

"And you Ms., I'm sorry, what was it?" he asked Natalie.

"Fisher. Natalie Fisher, sir."

"What did you see, Ms. Fisher?"

"Mr. Crew's account is accurate, Your Honor. I could tell that the probationer was angry when he entered the room. He began arguing with Mr. Crew before they even made it to his desk. He was attempting to intimidate…"

"Oh please, Your Honor," Smith interrupted yet again. "Is this witness a mind reader? How could she tell he was angry? How could she tell he was trying to be intimidating?"

"Your Honor," Natalie countered, "his voice was raised, the muscles in his neck were as tight as harp strings, and at one point, he jumped to his feet and leaned over Mr. Crew's desk, violating his personal space and..."

"I get it," the judge interjected. I think it's obvious, Ms. Smith. Your client threatened the probation officer."

"But, Your Honor..."

The judge looked over his glasses. "We are past this point, Counsel." He turned his attention back to Crew. "I'm absolutely convinced that he threatened you. Based on that, what is it you expect this court to do?"

Crew blurted out the final sentence of his supplemental report. "The court had sentenced the defendant to a lifetime term of probation in lieu of a prison term. As he has not adjusted to supervision, a term of incarceration is recommended."

"And what do you think, Ms. Fisher?"

"I think that the defendant is a safety risk to whatever agent he is assigned to. I know I wouldn't want to supervise him."

The judge leaned back, interlaced his fingers, and stretched his arms before pulling his hands back in his lap and leaning forward. "I wouldn't want to supervise him, either. But, you chose your profession and I chose mine." He turned his attention back to the defendant. "Be advised, young man, this type of behavior will not be tolerated. I will continue you on probation, on non-reporting status. Don't let me see you here again." The judge tapped his gavel and briskly left the courtroom.

## Chapter 40

"Look, it could be worse," Natalie consoled Crew as she pushed the down arrow on the elevator. "The judge could have believed his pack of lies."

"That's worse?" he asked in a dejected tone. "He believes us but he just doesn't care. I don't think that's better."

As Natalie prepared to respond, she noticed a familiar young girl scurry from the courtroom and down the hall. She was followed by a familiar-looking older woman. *Where do I know...*

Her thought was cut short by a face she wouldn't forget for quite some time. Eric James left the courtroom with his girlfriend. He was followed by the court-appointed probation officer for Judge Ash, Linda Lang. Lang walked toward the elevator while James and his girlfriend peered down at a piece of paper he was holding. Natalie's heart sank. It was a probation order.

The door opened and the three probation officers entered. Natalie broke the silence. "You're Lang, right?"

"That's right. I know I should know you. Sorry."

"Fisher. We met at new employee school."

"That's right. I've tried to block that time out of my mind. Weren't those trainers a real piece of work?"

"Ex-prison guards don't make the best teachers."

"Yeah. That quasi-military stuff is too much for me."

"No doubt," Natalie concurred as they entered the elevator. "Were you in the courtroom for the James sentencing?"

"Who?"

"The young guy who was standing by the door when you left."

Her look remained quizzical.

"It was a CSC. I saw the victim and her mother bolt out of there and..."

"Oh yeah. The judge sure couldn't please anyone there."

"What happened? I did the pre."

"You did the pre," she responded with a combination of excitement and surprise. "Oh my God! You should have heard some of the things his attorney said about you."

"Get out!" Crew laughed.

"No, really," she continued. "He tried to say you were biased. He picked your evaluation and plan apart. He went over the sentencing guideline scoring, point by point."

"Ouch. Just my luck. The first pre-sentence report in history that was actually read. So what was the damage? Does the judge think I'm a complete idiot?"

Lang laughed. "Trust me. By tomorrow, he won't remember your name. He let the guy rant a while, then he let the victim's mother do her impact statement, then he did what he planned on doing before you wrote your report and before he laid eyes on the victim or the defense attorney."

"What happened? I sure didn't expect to see him walk out of there. By statue, he should have done time."

"Yeah. They gave him a year in Dickerson, with work release. His attorney got the judge to delay his entry into county for a few weeks so he could get some things in order. It was crazy. You should have heard the girlfriend wail."

"A year in the county jail?"

"He'll do less than eight months with good time," Crew added.

"The judge upheld your guidelines, he just didn't follow them," Lang continued. "He gave him five years probation, first year county time and HYTA."

"He got HYTA. He had a shitload of priors. He didn't qualify for HYTA."

"Yeah. That's pretty much what the judge thought, but it seemed to be a real deal breaker. He didn't want the guy to withdraw his plea and start all over. He's got a hell of a docket as it is."

The elevator opened at the first floor.

"Hey," Lang concluded as she scooted out, "if you need anything, just give me a call. See you later."

"Open season," Crew grumbled.

"I'm sorry. What?"

"Open season," he repeated. "When the probationers learn that they can get out of reporting by threatening their PO, it'll be open season on us. Don't think shit like this doesn't get out in the lobby. They've got a hell of a grapevine." He took his keys from his jacket as they approached the row of glass doors leading out to the steps.

"Are you going back to the office or are you just gonna call it a day and head home?"

Natalie thought about the question as they stood on the steps. Her choices numbed her. An empty house. Another in what seemed to have become a bi-yearly ritual of dividing possessions. Or, there was the office. She could go and write another report that the judge would uphold, but disregard just to keep his docket moving.

It started to drizzle, and she was suddenly aware that Crew was still waiting for a response.

"I'm not sure."

"Well, I'm heading home. If you go back to the office, just tell 'em I'm at…oh hell, after today I don't care where you tell 'em I am."

"OK. But since I'm pretty sure you'll care more tomorrow, I'll tell them you went to the write-up room."

"Fine," he said as he turned up his collar and trotted down the stairs.

Outside, the sound of the flags snapping in the wind caught her attention. The colors seemed brighter against the gray backdrop of the sky. The wind picked up, and the drizzle turned to a full-fledged downpour. Natalie chuckled to herself as she descended the steps. *Enough already dad, I get it. Back to work!*

# About the Author

Alexis Janus graduated with a Bachelor's Degree in Social Work from Madonna University in 1991. She has been employed by The Michigan Department of Corrections as a felony Probation Officer for over 6 years. Her prior work experience in the fields of domestic violence and child welfare have provided her with a unique perspective on the treatment of felons and victims, as well as those who are paid to deal with them.

She wrote *Information and Belief* to provide the public with a behind the scenes view of the legal system.

She currently resides with her partner in Westland, Michigan.

Printed in the United States
767600003B